JOURNAL

MW01677993

bamboo ridge

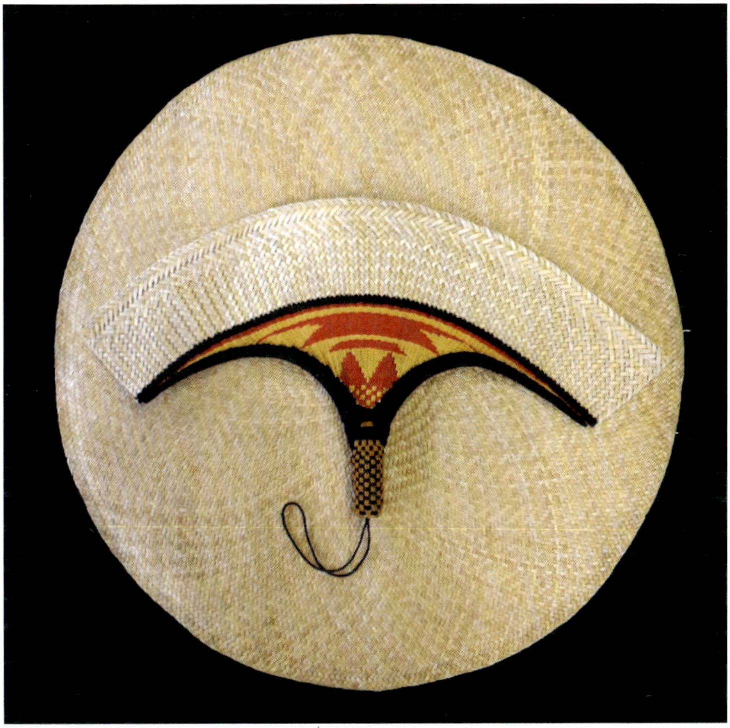

Issue No. 110

Bamboo Ridge Press

ISBN 978-0-910043-96-0
This is issue #110 (Fall 2016) of
Bamboo Ridge, Journal of Hawai'i Literature and Arts (ISSN 0733-0308)
Copyright © 2017 by Bamboo Ridge Press
All rights reserved. This book, or parts thereof,
may not be reproduced in any form without permission.
Published by Bamboo Ridge Press
Printed in the United States of America
Indexed in *Humanities International Complete*
Bamboo Ridge Press is a member of the
Community of Literary Magazines and Presses (CLMP).
Founding Editors: Eric Chock and Darrell H. Y. Lum
Guest Editors: Donald Carreira Ching and Misty-Lynn Sanico
Managing Editor: Joy Kobayashi-Cintrón
Copyeditor: Normie Salvador
Business Manager: Wing Tek Lum
Typesetting and design: Misty-Lynn Sanico
Cover design: Napunako Sanico
Cover art: *Pe'ahi Collection*, 2016, by Marques Hanalei Marzan
abaca cloth and pigment, 38" X 38"
Title page art: *Pe'ahimauliola*, 2016
Photos of art courtesy of artist

Bamboo Ridge Press is a nonprofit, tax-exempt corporation formed in 1978 to foster the appreciation, understanding, and creation of literary, visual, or performing arts by, for, or about Hawai'i's people. This publication was made possible with support from the National Endowment for the Arts (NEA) and the Hawai'i State Foundation on Culture and the Arts (SFCA), through appropriations from the Legislature of the State of Hawai'i (and grants from the NEA).

ART WORKS.

HAWAI'I
STATE FOUNDATION on
CULTURE and the ARTS

Bamboo Ridge is published twice a year.
For subscription information, back issues, or a catalog, please contact:
Bamboo Ridge Press; P.O. Box 61781; Honolulu, HI 96839-1781
808.626.1481; brinfo@bambooridge.com; www.bambooridge.com

Bamboo Ridge Press gratefully acknowledges the donations of the following individuals and organizations in 2016:

Jill Abbott
Carol Abe
Nancy Aleck
Robert A. Alm
Sherwin Alop
Anonymous (12)
Charles T. Araki
Esther Arinaga
Rita Ariyoshi
Cristina Bacchilega
Fred Bail
Barnes & Noble
Susan L. Becker
Emily A. Benton
Doreen E. Beyer
Joseph R. Bibeau
Teresa Bill
Dave Manu Bird
Amalia B. Bueno
The Cades Foundation
Jane Campbell
Vanessa K. Carter
Casey Charitable Matching Programs
Eric Chock
Ghislaine D. Chock
Sue Lin Chong
Sammie Choy
Xander Cintrón-Chai
Thomas Conger
Cathy Song Davenport
Kathleen Doering
Jackie Dudock
Suerte Dureg
Christina Dwight
Ernestine Enomoto
Elena Farden
Dimpna Figuracion
Foodland Super Market, Limited
Mark L. Forman
Cecily Fujii
Nicole Fujimoto
Joanna Glaser
Shiho Hamano
John Hara Associates, Inc.
Marie M. Hara
Mavis Hara
Gail Harada
Ermile Hargrove
Susan Harrison-Washington
Jim Harstad
Hawai'i Council for the Humanities
Hawai'i State Foundation on Culture and the Arts
Leonore Higa
Craig Howes
Judy Ilano
Janet Inamine
Roger Jellinek
Scott K. Kikkawa
Milton B. Kimura
Billy Kittredge
Joy Kobayashi-Cintrón
Brenda Kwon
Juliet Kono Lee
Lanning C. Lee
Sonia Leong
Michael Little
Eulalia Luckett
Jack Luckett
Daniel Lum
Darrell Lum
Mae Lum
Tan Tek Lum
Wing Tek Lum
Marion Lyman-Mersereau
Kasi Hara Mau
Michelle Moy
Audrey L. Mueh
Amy C. Murata
Lillian L. Nakamura
National Endowment for the Arts
Ethel Aiko Oda
Carol Ogino
Frances M. Oliver
Christy Passion
Patrick Patterson
PT
Terri M. Pule
Milton Sakuoka
Electa Sam
Liza Sanchez
Dan Seki
Harumi Serata
Eric Paul Shaffer
Stanley Shimoda
John Simonds
Michelle Cruz Skinner
George Smith
Sharon D. Smith
Susan Soong
Monica B. Sullivan
Julie Sy
Hazel H. Takumi Foundation
Larry Takumi
Noe Tanigawa
Kara Terada
Moriso Teraoka
Bill Teter
Delaina Thomas
Jean Toyama
Joe Tsujimoto
Amy L. Uyematsu
André Washington
Ruth L. Watabayashi
Western Union
David Wong
Eileen Wong
Susan Yim
Dana Yoshikane
Trisha Yoshizaki

CONTENTS

BAMBOO SHOOTS SELECTIONS

SPECIAL PREVIEW - *What We Must Remember*

EDITORS' NOTES

Donald:

I grew up in a household that discouraged pidgin with frozen chili peppers, where I learned to swallow the words before the ice melted. Later, in high school, Ms. Fujii at Castle High passed out photocopies of *The Best of Bamboo Ridge*, but I crumpled the pages up and kept my mouth shut. Or worse, spoke out with the same fiery condemnation that I had been taught years before. It wouldn't be until much later, when I started to read Rodney Morales and Lois-Ann Yamanaka in college, when I heard Eric Chock read "Poem for George Helm: Aloha Week 1980" on *Aloha Shorts*, when I realized that there were stories about Hawai'i that differed from those perpetuated in Waikīkī. It was then that I started to realize why Bamboo Ridge mattered so much. It was then that my tongue started to feel again.

Misty:

We left when I was four and didn't move back until I was thirteen. Growing up, pidgin was that funny thing my Dad spoke when we ran into other people from Hawai'i, or when he was telling us hanabata days stories. I wondered at the ease in which he could slip back and forth because pidgin always felt clumsy in my own mouth, like it didn't belong to me. I loved it anyway—the words, the cadence. Hearing pidgin meant "home" and a way to cling to it. But stories about Hawai'i, they were my lifeline.

The first time I read an issue of *Bamboo Ridge* it was like home. I saw aspects of myself and the people and places I love reflected back to me in other people's words, and realized the importance of perpetuating local literature.

Every issue of *Bamboo Ridge* is unique. This issue #110 was the first to accept electronic submissions. It was largely edited as a collaboration across one continent and two major oceans while Donald was living and writing abroad. Although it was a challenge, it came to symbolize the way that Bamboo Ridge's audience is growing, and the way that regional literature, Hawai'i literature, can have a global impact.

Donald:

This issue also stands out due to the mix of both emerging and established talent. Among familiar authors, you will find stories by writers who may have never been published in *Bamboo Ridge* before. As emerging authors ourselves, we feel that this is important. In addition, the list of contributors is diverse as are the themes throughout this issue. However, they were chosen because each provides a unique perspective and experience as well as insight into what local literature means today.

Misty:

Our featured artist, Marques Hanalei Marzan, uses native plants and other natural elements to create mesmerizing pieces of art, sculpture, and fashion. Similar to the way writers twist and arrange words, his intricate weaving and knotting is transformative, bringing new meaning, form, and purpose to raw material.

Donald:

Through his work, Marzan has found ways to weave traditional Native Hawaiian practices into the fabrics of modern art and design. His aesthetic tells his story as well as that of his families and his cultures, past and present. His pieces are deeply rooted in these things and in Hawai'i, and it is an honor to share his work in this issue.

We hope you enjoy these offerings. Mahalo for supporting Hawai'i literature and art.

Donald Carreira Ching
Misty-Lynn Sanico

ARTIST PROFILE & PORTFOLIO

Marques Hanalei Marzan

Photo credit: Kai Markell, 2016

Marques Hanalei Marzan is a fiber artist, a Native Hawaiian cultural practitioner, and cultural advisor accomplished in hula and chant as well as weaving. His sculpture and wearable art is created using indigenous or early Polynesian materials, many of which he cultivates or processes himself. He uses shape, pattern, and layers to explore concepts of Hawaii's past, present, and future.

Visit his website for more: www.marquesmarzan.com

Lynn Cook

Dream Weaver

Marques Hanalei Marzan weaves history, is inspired by history, and is creating new history. Galleries, workshops, shopping centers, fashion runways, museums—no matter who you are or where you see his unforgettable artistry, it's a paradoxical experience of time and texture. What you see is both ancient and modern, universal and Hawaiian.

Imagine a young Hawaiian boy, growing up in the ahupuaʻa of Kāneʻohe on the island of Oʻahu. His list of pursuits played like a Disney movie—swim, fish, garden, climb a mountain; and he did. But the most important thing he did was watch. Many island kids are taught to do that—be quiet, watch, and listen—to the waves, the clouds, and their kūpuna. He says his fascination with weaving started early, looking at family heirloom lau hala hats stored away in the cupboard, amazed by their intricacies and fineness.

Surrounded by an encouraging family, Marzan loved to draw. He made mud pots and dried them with the vent on the clothes dryer. He made paper. He listened to stories about his grandfather, who fished in the morning and made nets in the afternoon, and his great-grandmother who made quilts and wove lau hala, plaiting the long leaves and planting a seed of wonder in a young Marzan. Knots, and weaving, and sewing.

The family quilts he speaks of were made in the Hawaiian tradition, a design cut from one single large piece of fabric, carefully basted and stitched to solid white background and then quilted.

"I didn't know what the pattern was or why she made it. My Aunty's answer to me was, 'you'll figure it out.'"

He got the same answer about lau hala weaving and many other Hawaiian practices—possibly the answers that would set him on his voyage of discovery. Thread, cord, feathers, fabric, and lauhala weaving inspired his imagination, Marzan says, far more than biology class or any other high school activities.

"When I was in high school, the daughter of my mom's co-worker and I decided to take a lau hala weaving class. It was a 'why not?' moment so I signed on. I was hooked!"

His flashback moment was remembering the stories of his great-grandmother's hands as her fingers flew, weaving the thin strips of lau hala into works of art.

Marzan graduated from Castle High School and went on to the University of Hawai'i at Mānoa as a biology major—a bit of a reach from weaving. There, a professor already known as the Pied Piper of fiber, Maile Andrade, check-marked his name on the list of students in her "Introduction to Fiber" class. Shortly thereafter Marzan changed his major to art, specifically fiber.

A connection with Pat Hickman at the University of Hawai'i led to a course in textile conservation and an internship at the Bishop Museum in Honolulu. It was during this time that Marzan began to expand his textile experience, following the Northwest Coast native tribal influence on Hickman, learning to use hog intestines, the na'au.

His first big project as an intern was to inventory the makaloa mats in the museum's collection.

"I kept volunteering. They found more for me to do and finally I got a job as a collections technician."

When the Bishop Museum Hawaiian Hall was closed for renovations, the hale pili, grass house, was de-constructed and re-constructed by conservation experts. At the end of their basic restoration the team left, but Marzan stood in the Hall, knowing that more details needed to be attended to. He simply did what he knew what was right and spent many nights all by himself perched on the scaffolding surrounding the house, weaving in the last of the dried pili grass, harvested from the slopes of Mauna Kea, attaching each bundle high up on the roof of the hale.

He says the hale is the piko of the museum, what the Western world calls the belly button, the umbilical connection to life. One morning, he realized that the hale floor mat had not been replaced, and decided to make a new one. Though the hale is only to view, and not to step inside, he knew the house would not be finished without it. With his access to historic photos and notes, he was able to weave an 8-by-10-foot lau hala floor mat in the same technique as the original, and completed it in time for the opening ceremonies. He laughs when local folks who know, smile and hum a few bars of the song by Iz "Hawaiian Superman." Quietly humble about his role in bringing life back into the hale, Marques does admit that he was truly honored and blessed to see it to its completion.

More creative opportunity came when Kumu Hula Victoria Holt Takamine dreamed of an event to honor Hawaiian artists who perpetuate the Hawaiian culture. She organized a month-long celebration in May, dubbed Maoli Arts Month, MAMo. Loving the outrageous and fantastic creations by her friend, Marques Hanalei Marzan, she invited him to participate. Soon enough the MAMo runway show became the Hawai'i version of Paris Fashion Week. Weaving and printing and creating as he does on his living room floor, Marzan's fashions were and continue to be wonderfully over the top with capes of dried pig gut and hair accessories that defy gravity.

Ultimately he says his parents raised him, and his brothers, to do what they enjoy. "Don't worry about making money, be happy at what you do," they said, knowing full well that loving what you do is a life plan, a career. He followed their advice and describes his life as "whatever comes across my path. I never try to make something, I just try to keep my mind open and hands free so that things happen. I let things be what they want to be."

What has happened in his art life covers many bio-pages. The list includes numerous awards and exhibitions, plus presentations across the globe from Paris to New Zealand describing methods of weaving, explaining things like "binding, looping, and the magic of Jaki-Ed: Marshallese Mats." It is a fact that many Hawai'i artists suggest, "If you want to know what it is and how it is done, ask Marques."

"I just share what I know or am learning."

There are times when Marques Hanalei Marzan teaches. Those lucky enough to attend his class soon find that they must make a promise, "When I teach you, you can't keep it for yourself. First understand how to do it and then pass it on."

Self Portrait (2006) Bamboo, split reed, hibiscus fiber, paper, and hemp.

Lines in Time (2002) Split reed, bamboo, paper, makaloa, bulrush, pandanus, and hemp.

Hānau ʻia (2000) Natural and dyed pandanus

Pe'ahi Collection (2016) Abaca cloth, coconut sennit, hemp cord, cotton cord, split reed, and pigment

Pe'ahi Collection (2016) Abaca cloth, coconut sennit, hemp cord, cotton cord, split reed, and pigment

Pe'ahi Collection (2016) Abaca cloth, coconut sennit, hemp cord, cotton cord, split reed, and pigment

REBOOT Installation (2016) Leather, abaca cloth, bamboo beads, felt, cotton fabric, and pigment

REBOOT Installation (2016) Leather, abaca cloth, bamboo beads, felt, cotton fabric, and pigment

Pe'ahi Collection (2016) Abaca cloth, coconut sennit, hemp cord, cotton cord, split reed, and pigment

Joe Balaz

Eating Lunch Wit Siddhartha

Da past
is wun stale manapua.

Now
is wun hot laulau.

Tomorrow
is like dreaming about kulolo.

Da idea

is to just enjoy da food
dat stay on da plate in front of you.

You not going starve, brah,
so no be down wit wun frown.

No pilikia.
No worry too much.

No need have
dat nervous mynah bird

always yapping in your ear.

Try foa downshift
and simply savor da current flavor
in your very own

day to day personal luau.

Buddha said—

"The past is already gone,
the future is not yet here.

There's only one moment for you to live,
and that is the present moment."

Dat buggah wuz wise

and I bet
he really knew how foa eat too.

In da cafeteria

me and his spirit would really dine and grind
wenevah dey had Spanish Rice on da menu.

Siddhartha, brah—

I read all about him
in one of my senior classes in high school.

Wen I stay hungry
I apply his philosophy

and I find nirvana
every time I chow down.

Natalia Fernandez

Idyllwild

There was snow moving in. It was one of those rare Southern California days that turn the mountains white and every landscape into a postcard. On days like this the locals stay indoors, old people's joints cramp with rheumatic pain and the lucky weekenders get their money's worth.

Peter and his wife were entering a cabin they had rented online when feathery ice crystals started dropping from the sky. A good omen, Peter thought, since there was seldom any weather in LA where they lived and he sometimes missed it. He felt welcomed, reassured, hopeful for their long weekend away. Coming had been a good idea.

He wasn't even through with this thought when Anna tripped on the awkward step separating the kitchen from the living room. Regaining her footing, she stretched out an arm to stop him where he stood, a few steps behind her.

"Someone's here," she said.

She was trying to make sense of something she was hearing, some noise that Peter figured was coming from deep inside the cabin.

He had been the one to book the place and all his brain had to anticipate its layout were the pictures from the ad. From the photos he remembered a full-size master bedroom with an attached bathroom, another good-sized bedroom, a living room and a breakfast nook, a kitchen of course, and then another bedroom, this one tiny and with a bed built into it in a way that resembled a boat's cabin. There was also an outdoor hot tub on the deck, a selling point for Peter, but all this information was useless. He couldn't tell where each thing was, not from the kitchen where they were still standing.

"Over there," Anna whispered, pointing to the east side of the cabin. "You hear it?"

He couldn't hear a thing and it wasn't new. The ringing in his ears had only grown louder with age. He had recently turned forty-five and it had hit him like a blow. "Halfway to ninety," his friends teased him. They were all the same age, but Peter took it to heart. His children were still young; he couldn't bear the idea of missing their future. And what had he ever done with his life? He felt the weight of his once imagined future, this present of his, different from what he had expected, that future that came so fast and to stay. His life had gone so quickly, he thought, looking about the cabin for a clue as to what to do next.

He had been married to Anna for a decade, though he never used the word "decade" in relation to marriage. He was a linguistics professor, words mattered to him, so while he didn't object to the noun itself, the Greek prefix seemed to mask the passage of time in a manner that he disliked. Ten years seemed a more accurate way to refer to their shared history. "We've been married ten years," he would say with pride when introducing Anna to strangers, "ten whole years." And during those years, they had built a comfortable sense of intimacy strengthened by their three children, the dog, the house, the deep knowledge of each other's biographies. Then on a day like no other, a day that wasn't a day but several days lumped together, a sense of peril had appeared and with it came uncertainty. Aware of it, Peter had insisted on a trip. So now the kids were home with grandma and the two of them in a cabin for their first vacation alone since their first child was born.

Peter knew, like one does when inserting himself in the bigger picture of the world, that all these details were mundane. Yet to him this life was the universe. These were facts, his facts, stored somewhere in his mind, facts he could easily access as indeed he did while standing by his wife, confronted with the idea of facing an intruder.

Idyllwild had been his choice. She wanted a warmer place, or so he imagined. Would she have preferred Palm Springs? He couldn't tell and she hadn't said. He had hoped it'd be like old times, whatever his brain meant by this. He didn't question his brain often. He knew what it meant even when he didn't. And Idyllwild had been the ground of their untested hopes. They used to come before the children, pack an overnight bag and hit the road Friday after his last class, back on Sunday night or even Monday morning, straight to campus feeling great, the memory of her naked body still fresh on his mind, a goofy smile on his face, beaming.

"Maybe we should leave," he offered. "I'll call the rental place and explain the situation."

But it was too late. Anna was already in the living room and he behind her, trying to make sense of her sudden display of bravery, almost excited for it.

He caught up with her again in the hallway.

"I hear the noise now," he said. "I do."

"Good for you, old man." A joke, since she was five years his junior and often reminded him of it.

Then her face changed again and Peter couldn't tell if it now showed fear or bravado. She whispered to him to stand still and be quiet.

In a second she was gone, lost behind a door Peter imagined led to one of the bedrooms. Once more he was forced to act, pick a course of action, move, not move, keep existing here and now.

He couldn't tell what came first, his entering the room or Anna's voice, but he knew what she meant when he saw what she saw: six furry things curled up in the corner of the room, staring right at them.

"Are these raccoons?" he asked, knowing the answer.

Anna was already by their side.

"Baby raccoons," she said, picking one up.

He noticed the smile on her face, broad, full of teeth, a long-forgotten smile, the one from before. She brought the furry animal up to her cheek to feel its softness and closed her eyes in delight.

"They're called kits," he said in the same tone of voice he used to lecture his students. "Some call them cubs, but I prefer the word kit."

"You're so lucky we're here," Anna said to the raccoons, and then to Peter: "I'll get them some food."

She went to the van to raid their snacks and when she came back, Peter was still standing where she had left him. Where were the kits' parents, he wondered, as they devoured the crumbs Anna cupped in her hand. They seemed well fed and healthy, a fact that made him conclude the kits had been nursed.

He was about to speak when he noticed Anna's expression, her white smile seemingly broadening, if that was even possible, becoming so big as to take over her face.

"What are we going to do with them?" he asked.

"What do you mean what are we going to do? Aren't they adorable?"

"We can't just…we can't just let them be here," he heard himself say.

"Why?"

He had no answers. The crumbs gone, the kits still looked for Anna's hand, seeking to be petted and cradled. She swapped the kit she was holding for a smaller one.

"I'm going to go get the bags," Peter said at last, leaving the room unnoticed.

Anna had been playing with the kits since getting to the cabin—it was trying Peter's patience. It wasn't that he didn't care about them. He had to admit that they were cute too, but his brain always went for the logistics. It was perhaps the father in him, or the thing before the children that made it so he could become a father, the thing at the core of it all. He was a problem-solver and his instinct was to find out as much as he could about what to do with the kits. Crackers didn't seem an appropriate meal. And would a pet shelter take them? Then there was the issue of the cabin's owner, who Peter imagined would want to know what was happening. There was so much to consider.

"Should we go for a walk?" he asked, putting his mind to rest.

"I'm kind of tired from the drive," Anna said.

She was on her phone an hour later and Peter on the couch. He had brought *Amphigorey* for the trip and was moving his eyes over it, the meaning of sentences lost, the pictures sticking to his brain.

Someone had recommended it to him, he couldn't remember who or when, only that it had been on his radar for years. Then at long last, when taking his oldest to the library for the latest Harry Potter, he had remembered to look for it.

He was enjoying it all right, even if at times he felt too old to be reading this type of book. He turned another page and was taken by the perplexed ink faces of people on a staircase. They were looking off at a strange creature wearing a scarf. The creature had just appeared there and something was clearly wrong. The whole scene was unsettling.

He noticed Anna across the room—she was texting. Could she be writing the children? The kids were too young to text, but they had recently set up an email account for their oldest son and made a point of messaging him sometimes. She could be doing that. Or texting a friend. Or her mother. Peter could only hope.

Against his better judgment, he watched her fingers on the screen, then his book, then her fingers again. At last giving him a rest, she put the phone down and shifted her attention back to one of the kits. She played with it for a moment and then, as if answering an urgent calling, she left the room.

Peter's eyes were instantly on the unattended cell phone. He felt his heart rate accelerate. A thin line of sweat trailed down his forehead. He was incredibly cold.

Left behind on the table, the kit was also taken by the phone. Its dainty little hands were trying to pick it up, lousily attempting to get a grip on it. Peter had to admit it was a comical sighting.

He took a longer than average breath in attempting to regain control of himself. Some time between the moment he decided to walk up to the phone and the moment he actually stood up, Anna came back.

He stopped mid-motion, like his kids did when caught raiding the candy bowl. She must have sensed something, seen the weird look on his face, the awkward position of his legs, because in no time she pocketed the phone, picked up the kit, and left the room again.

He found her later in the kits' room, still playing with them. That's what they were calling it now, the kits' room, since the raccoons had unofficially taken over it. It was the back room, the one that looked the biggest in the online photos. Peter couldn't tell how long the kits had been there, or when the last time was that someone had aired out the house, only that the kits' room had taken on their scent, the result a stuffy raccoon stench.

The door was slightly ajar and Anna on the floor, three kits crawling over her crossed legs, the others sniffing around her scarf.

"They're incredibly smart," she said when Peter entered. "This one's my favorite," she added, lifting up a kit before burying her nose in its fur. "He has this little white patch here, can you see it?"

Peter was distracted by the purring. Did raccoons purr? He wasn't sure what the proper verb was though he was almost certain that they were making a weird humming sound. He made a mental note to look it up later.

"I'm going to call the kids," he said, leaving the room, all the while wondering if he should be doing something about the raccoons.

His mother-in-law put his oldest on the phone. Miles was eight and had only recently started to indulge them by getting on the line.

"How's it going, buddy?"

"Goooood," the kid said, in a funny voice.

"What are you doing?"

"Just playing on my tablet."

"Yeah? Which game?"

"The hotel one."

"Nice. Are the Millers still there?"

"Yeah. Well, they had a daughter and now she moved out," Miles said.

"I thought they had just gotten married."

"Yeah, but then they had a baby and now she is old."

"Oh. Did you have lunch yet?"

"Yes. Grandma made pasta. She says I have to go. Bye, Daddy."

Miles got off the line and Peter's mother-in-law came back on.

"You should go enjoy yourselves; everything is fine here," she said, rushing him off the phone.

Peter was annoyed. This was his kid for god's sake; he was enjoying himself.

He got off the phone and thought of the Millers. Miles had recently gotten this game where he was an apartment manager, even though he called the building a hotel. Peter found the misnomer endearing and loved hearing all about it. In the game, Miles had to name the tenants and furnish their apartments. Dave Miller was Peter's favorite. He had asked Miles about the name choice but all the kid said was that he had just thought of it. Something about the randomness of the name cracked Peter up. And now the Millers had a daughter! And she was old enough to leave! A bout of sadness came over him. Not the Millers, he thought, and for a second it felt as if the whole world was going.

"What time is it?" Anna asked.

"A quarter to eight. Why?"

They were driving back from a steak dinner at a bistro where the intense fireplace heat had flushed Peter's cheeks. He put the window down to let the icy wind in.

"My phone's dead. Why are you stopping?"

"Let's get a nightcap," he said, pulling over in front of a small bar.

"What about the raccoons? What if they need me?"

"They'll be fine."

"No, let's just go back."

"Don't be silly," he said, turning off the engine. "They're fine."

Things escalated quickly. A moment later, she was off the van walking in the direction of the cabin, the wind swinging her from left to right. He watched her walk away, just a thin black line in a wide white night, her feet sinking into the snow.

She was on the phone when he got back to the cabin. At the

sight of him, she walked into the kits' room, closed the door, and stayed there until the next morning.

That night the cabin rattled. Heavy snow came down at midnight and hit the windows like darts. A cool wind snuck in. The hot tub's loose cover was banging against the deck's railing and sometime around two Peter woke up on the couch and went to secure it.

He made it across the slippery deck without falling and was able to close the hot tub without much trouble. The cool air reddened his bare arms and legs. Under his feet, the packed ice stuck to his soles. With the job done, he closed his eyes and took in the silent night. It was as if the world were empty, devoid of all people and things. This was a recurrent thought, one that popped into his mind whenever he was up late while most people slept. Tonight, to his own surprise, he found the thought soothing, almost appealing.

The next morning he was sick. He woke up damp with sweat, cold to the core, and shivering.

"What's wrong?" Anna asked when he found her sitting at the breakfast nook, a cup of coffee and a book before her, one of the kits curled up on her lap.

"I don't feel well."

"Did you take something?"

He hadn't yet.

Anna was feeding toast to the kit. The sight of its small hands gripping the food haunted Peter.

"Should they be having human food?" he asked.

"They seem to like it," she said.

Peter went to the kitchen for a cup of coffee. He was struggling to breathe. When he came back, Anna noticed he looked pale.

"You don't look good. You should probably go back to bed," she offered.

The coffee was soothing his mouth and activating his brain. Another shiver shook his body and he wished he had put on a heavier sweater, but walking back to the bedroom to change seemed like a lot of work. When he got up for a second cup, he felt his knees wobbling, and all the way to the kitchen his walk was unsteady. Through the pain, he heard Anna's voice—she wanted a refill, too. With effort, he threaded his way back to retrieve her empty mug. By the time he returned with the fresh coffee his forehead was lined with cold sweat.

Later that day he had a fever dream.

He was descending some grandiose stairs in one of those high-ceiling palaces only known to him through movies and children's books. On recognizing that he was wearing old-fashioned long johns he felt embarrassed and self-aware, and under his bare feet the marble floors felt icy cold. A heavy, full-length fur coat, perfectly shaped and standing up, started moving toward him and it took Peter a moment to realize that the coat wasn't moving of its own accord but that an old bearded man was wearing it.

An air of familiarity surrounded this ominous man, though even in the dream Peter realized he didn't know him. The uneasiness that the man brought forth was a fully formed anxiety and, actualizing Peter's fears, the bearded man assaulted him.

Then they were in a narrow corridor and coming in contact with the fur Peter could have sworn that the coat itself was alive. He gasped for air, instead taking in a mouthful of fur. The coat was chocking him. The fur was all the way down his throat and he gagged, kicked his legs, and swung his fists to fight the coat. But his efforts would be in vain. This was happening because of who the man was—Peter just happened to be there. He could sense this in the way of dreams, with a full-force certainty that seems to precede the situation it refers to without predicting it. Nothing Peter could do would stop the man.

The windows blew open with an icy draft. It was the late afternoon. Peter sprang to attention and wrenched his body out of bed, seizing his glasses from the nightstand. They were his doctor's answer to presbyopia and though they only helped with reading, he put them on hoping to make sense of the figure that, across from him, was staring in his direction.

For a split second, he wondered if he was still asleep—though he was not—or whether the dream, which had adversely impacted his mood, was having in him also a hallucinogenic effect. Both thoughts discarded, he had to concede that this was real life and that the full-grown raccoon sniffing his shoe was, well, a raccoon sniffing his shoe.

He called out for his wife.

His shrill cry was followed by a coughing fit. He wasn't scared by this new raccoon, it wasn't about fear, but waking up had not quite erased from his mind the impression made by his dream and the presence of yet another uninvited guest seemed to restore it somehow.

He called for Anna again, perhaps hoping that outnumbering the raccoon would make it go away, or simply wanting someone else to attest to its actual presence.

For the first time now, the raccoon seemed aware of Peter. Its stark eyes were perusing his face, giving him the opportunity to do the same. Taking off his glasses—they were of no help at all—his eyes took in the distinctive black fur around the raccoon's eyes, the thin long whiskers, the dexterous front paws holding on to his Paul Evans.

As if breaking a spell, a moment of silent communion with the creature, Peter reached for a pair of pants lying across a chair and with much effort, for his lungs were fighting another coughing fit, he started to get dressed.

"Shoo!" he cried to the raccoon once he was able to refill his lungs with enough air. But what for? The creature was probably back for the kits.

He left the room almost ashamed. Unlike the bedroom, the rest of the cabin conformed to his idea of reality and he welcomed this familiarity with a deep, melancholy sigh. Anna seemed to be out, and with another sigh, this one heavy and unconscious, his mind began its maniacal spinning.

Where in the world could she be, he found himself thinking, like there was no store nearby, no town a mere minutes away where she could be shopping, no mountains to hike, like he was some sort of alien for whom unscheduled outings were hard to comprehend.

He came at last to the breakfast nook where they had sat

together that morning and, taking the same seat he had taken earlier, he struggled to think back on his dream. He aimed to organize its contents in a real-life chronology, but like all dream-events, what he remembered resisted this kind of arrangement. He recognized that meaning—that coveted prize—would likely elude him, but striving for it was a cause worth his time.

He was forced to abandon the task a few minutes later when he heard the front door. The impression the dream had made on him was not as easy to dispel as his concentration, but at last easing worry from his face, he got up to help his wife put groceries away.

Their stay in the cabin was split in half by the return of the kits' mother. Happy to eat off Anna's hand, eager for crumbs and crackers and table scraps, the kits had lost all interest in nursing and were now going unfed.

The mother raccoon had taken to the kits' room and reestablished its domain. The door ajar, the creature seemed to be guarding the room's entrance and every time Peter walked down the hallway, he did it under the raccoon's severe gaze. He wished he could convey his friendliness. He was relieved to know that the mother would be there to feed the kits once their stay was over, even if at present the kits weren't cooperating. Many times he found himself setting his face to a welcoming expression that he believed would send the right message, and every time he encountered the same defiant raccoon eyes.

Anna didn't seem happy with the change. The moment he told her the news he saw something on her face, a hint of disdain written on her brow that showed she didn't approve. He tried to console her, if consoling was indeed what she needed.

"The raccoon will take better care of them than we could," he said.

Anna didn't seem to hear him, or mind him. She was off to the kits' room, her rushed feet on the soundless carpet, arms swinging back and forth and increasing her speed.

Peter remained on the couch where he had been sitting for the past hour.

A few minutes later Anna was back.

"They don't seem to like that raccoon very much," she sentenced. "I'm not even sure that's their mother."

She sat on the chair across from Peter.

"I don't know," he said. "I think it is."

"Why would you say that? You always want to argue with me."

He recognized her tone, the prelude of an argument. As stealthily as possible, he turned his eyes back to his book.

"I'm going to read some more before dinner," he said.

He heard her loud sigh and sensed she was getting upset. But what could he possibly do? He turned to the page, reading a sentence that insisted on dancing across the page.

The next day was more or less uneventful. Peter talked Anna into using the hot tub and they spent most of the afternoon sitting there. Since their last and only conversation about it, he had become weary of any mention of the kits and, for the sake of marital harmony, he had avoided the subject. He knew he shouldn't bring it up, yet he wished he could talk things through with her, convey his worry that their intrusion in the cabin had put the kits at risk.

He wondered how long the kits could go without food and made a point to look it up later. If technology provided nothing else, it allowed for the certainty that no matter how random the question, someone has already asked it online.

The strong sun was down the horizon, dyeing the snow a deep, dark red. He followed Anna out of the hot tub and indoors to the comfort of the fireplace. The shuffling sound of kits came down the hallway. They were still in the back room, where they had been since the start, and stealing a glance at his wife Peter wondered if she would try to go into the room again. She hadn't attempted it since the mother raccoon had shown up and it was almost as if she had lost all interest in the furry creatures.

He saw her turn the corner and go into the master bedroom.

That night Peter was beginning to feel better, the coughing fits a thing of the past. He decided to make fettuccine Alfredo and, used to measuring for five portions, he miscalculated how much the two of them could possibly eat. They had brought a bottle of Prisoner from home—expensive enough that having it was a bit of a treat—and, looking to turn the night into an occasion, he decided to open it.

After dinner, they sat on the couch drinking from mismatched glasses Peter had fished out of the back of a cabinet. His was a dull shade of green, a thick, gaudy chalice. He had given her the better one, a thin, stemless glass resembling the ones they had at home. With a fire going, Peter wished their dog were there. Rocco loved fireplaces but Anna had decided it was too much work to bring him. Perhaps it was for the better, Peter thought, since the children would have missed him way too much. He couldn't wait to see all of them again, the children, the dog. He liked his life all right. He was lucky.

The first glass finished, Anna asked for a refill. They were talking animatedly about something of little practical importance to their lives: the improbable mass of neutrinos. Neither of them had any scientific background, but Anna had read an article about the mysterious particle and was trying to explain to him why it mattered that they had mass after all. Peter gathered this was somehow a contested issue, though he couldn't figure out why, or why his wife seemed so interested. She had that sometimes, interests that came and went quickly. By the time he was able to catch up to it, she had usually moved on to something else. He gave the neutrinos another week or two, and only half-listening he focused on the sweet taste of wine.

The bottle gone, he found himself yawning. And content. On the way to the bedroom, Anna lost her footing and, with as much chivalry as he had left, he offered his arm for support. They entered the dark room with their arms linked together, stumbling onto bed fully clothed.

Only now, seeing his wife surrender control to the powerful gods of alcohol, he remembered that earlier in the day he had figured out the passcode to her phone.

1438, his brain offered. 1438, it insisted. 1438. 1438. 1438. He didn't want to remember. But he didn't want to forget.

He glanced at her in the half shadow of the bedroom. Her eyes were closed, a lock of hair lawlessly across her face, the phone loosely gripped on her right hand. He gently tucked her hair behind her ears, all the while ignoring his impertinent brain as it offered a number he was trying to forget. Anna's fingers loosened the grip on the phone even more and he inhaled a deep, long breath, filling his lungs to capacity and hoping to buy himself enough time to let the impulse die out.

Then Anna's drowsy eyes opened. She seemed confused by her surroundings, as if the brief sleep had erased from her mind all memory of her being in the cabin. Peter was trying to soothe her by running a hand over her hair when a dormant urge took over him.

His wants had always been sudden. The process went something like this: without even a hint of a buildup, something inside him reached a boiling point. And that was that. It was always kind of shocking.

He took Anna in his arms easing the sleep from her face, letting his mental processes die at the hands of his animal instincts. And she welcomed it—how surprising that she would, how new all over again. It was a vestige of their earlier years when things felt urgent, a time when she was his, of her own accord, and likewise he had belonged to her.

He was on top of her now, kissing her neck and irritating her skin with the days-long beard of which he became physically aware. But she didn't seem to mind the beard. She even seemed to like it.

He undressed her quickly, feeling like a body that in the present tense possessed no thoughts, and moving his hand over Anna's back, he was fully taken by the pleasant sensation. He hugged her tightly, digging his short nails into her back, pressing her body against his.

The room was completely dark. All he could see was Anna's shape, the contours of her head, her slender limbs, and messy hair. Inside of her there was no time, no world, no reality. His legs began to cramp, but he couldn't stop. He didn't want to stop. And she was panting.

When it was over, he collapsed in bed and fell asleep at once.

The next morning was their last in the cabin. They had coffee at the breakfast nook, Anna browsing an outdated Idyllwild brochure and Peter finishing his book. He liked this about trips, his ability to get through an entire book as if it were in one sitting, the pages flowing as the writer intended, not too many days inconveniently squeezed between them.

Amphigorey was having an impression on him, and once more he wished he could remember which one of his friends had recommended it. For all he knew it was someone he no longer saw. Friendships had changed with the arrival of the children, so many years ago at this point, and as if put through a colander, only friends of a certain quality had remained. He didn't feel too sad about this, it was only natural, he thought.

He was eager to see his children—it had been too long. They were probably still in bed, he thought, confirming with his watch that only Lola, their youngest, would be up. She had once told him she liked when everyone else slept because she could hear the sounds of her brain. She was three and a half and had him wrapped around her finger, a fact he often bragged about.

He fidgeted on his seat. The events of the previous night had brought on a certain level of serenity, yet anticipating the drive back he felt anxious. He looked in the direction of Anna, who didn't notice his glancing. They hadn't mentioned the kits since the mother raccoon's appearance and he didn't think his wife had but once gone into the kits' room. It was like having renters in a guesthouse, renters they never saw but of which they were aware all the time.

"What about the kits?" he asked, almost against his will.

"What about them?" Anna said, her eyes buried in the brochure.

"What's going to happen to them once we're gone?"

"They're with their mother now," she said, and Peter heard this as one would a sentence at trial.

"I thought you didn't think it was their mother," he said.

"It is."

With that, she ended the conversation.

Peter had been mindlessly crushing a piece of toast and opening his hand he saw the crumbs stack to his palm.

He hadn't been in the kits' room since the mother's reappearance and if he was being honest with himself he wasn't too pleased to have to do it again. But someone had to.

The door was still ajar and walking down the hallway he noticed the raccoon's eyes on him. It was on top of the bed, the kits away from it, curled up together in the corner of the room. It was an odd sighting and the distance between them struck him as inconceivable. He tried to think of his children, of how they would feel if they were abandoned, not that it was the same or a nice thought to entertain. And it wasn't just the few feet separating the kits from their parent that made him uneasy, there was something else, something more, a distance that wasn't physical but that was still visible. This was a kingdom he didn't understand, an order that was foreign to him, where a parent could be so removed from its offspring. He didn't have to get it, he finally accepted. It wasn't his place to get it.

He hurried his pace and swung the door open. Aware of having put the mother raccoon on high alert Peter rushed to the kits' side, opened his hand and watched their hungry mouths devour the crumbs. He felt the raccoon's eyes on his back but didn't turn to face it. When the kits were done feeding, he left the room as quickly as he had entered, only to return later, right before leaving the cabin, to drop off a full loaf of bread.

This last feeding done, he was closing the door to the kits' room when a forming thought presented itself, the prelude of a wave that would later drown him and against which he had no power—his wife was going to leave him.

He didn't know where this untimely thought was coming from, or why. All he knew was that he wasn't projecting the kits' plight onto his own life and that the thought was just there, the same way his hands were now on the luggage, his boots on the snow, his wife still inside the cabin. The thought was there, nothing to do about it.

He felt it as if he could physically experience it. The seasons would fold, one into another in a meaningless chronology, and time—that grim enforcer—would tally its victims. He would age even more and with diminishing abilities live in a world he won't understand. And Anna won't be there. As inconceivable as it seemed, she would not be by his side, she would choose not to be. And as a beautiful woman discovers her first gray hair and knackered bachelors become fathers he too would be forced to live, to remain, pushed into an unimagined future he would face for his children's sake, and for his own, in that order. And it would be backbreaking, he could feel it already, unthinkable and unjustifiable, a death by fire, an execution.

At this precise moment he saw her clearly too, as if she had just walked into focus. A hard yellow figure leaving the cabin, carved against the white winter. He noticed her light brown hair and close-grained skin. Her wrinkles like deep furrows. Her limbs that pushed out of her torso as if sprouting from rotten stumps. And then nothing underneath it, none of the elementary particles he had once recognized. He saw this figure get in the van and fasten her seatbelt as if readying herself for battle.

He stood still, unable or unwilling to move and exist in any other space but the one in which he was. Some minutes passed and then the wind grew stronger, making the gray cashmere scarf slap his face.

She seemed to be texting when he made the decision. He would not start the van. He would refuse to go home. Home. The word seemed to mock him now. He would not brush his teeth thinking of nothing. He would not share a bed with her. He would not undress like he had no flaws to hide. He would not be sound asleep when morning wins over night. He would not wake up and have coffee like on any other morning. The children won't see them and know. The future won't come.

And then he moved again, letting his legs do all the work, and in no time he was driving away from the cabin and the raccoons and the thoughts—the thoughts, they were the trouble. They felt foreign to him now. The reality of his hands on the steering wheel and his body on the driver's seat taking over, these inconceivable thoughts that had felt so final, so possible and impossible at the same time, were now a sign that he might be losing his mind. Had he spun into panic based on a hunch? Was he being unfair to his wife? He couldn't tell and it troubled him.

He watched her once more, her eyes closing as she drifted into sleep, her phone momentarily unattended. And he could unlock it. He could see for himself, mitigate or fuel his fears. He could reach for it without even pulling over. He could know.

The sun was starting to set and he was eager to see the kids. His brain's attention split between Anna's phone and the thought of his children, the anticipation of hugs and kisses. He wondered how they had been, what they'd eaten for lunch. Rush hour would fizzle out by the time they hit LA. They could be back before the kids' bedtime. He was hoping for that.

When Anna's phone vibrated with an incoming text, Peter perused her face, out of reach in the country of sleep, and determined she was unaware.

His eyes were now on the screen, the message bright and clear. Against his better judgment, he reached for her phone and unlocked it.

Joseph Han

Grey Hair Song

for Hyun Ja Han

The pansori singer's prelude
    flows a clear stream

    into a high pitched mountain—
    forced to blossom from

    her voice—

~

Shall I kill myself to become a swallow

and build a nest near my lover's home?

How shall I live in the trees and weep

alone? Even the leaves will abandon me

~

Listen to the drum, the cowhide's pulse.
It paves the road for her song
as the earth turns, four ways
of rhythm and tone:

push
add
cut
undo

~

When her song weeps with grief,
the drumbeat weakens with old age.

~

When silence lingers from the tip
of an exhale, the drum must sever.

~

Let's live this world with ease.

A man does not live for hundreds

of years. My dear love is gone

in a flock of wild geese.

They carry him to the clouds.

~

she sings
for a dead husband

from intestines filled with sorrow
and draped by kudzu vines.

Her voice follows changing
seasons, from fragrant

grasses to snow.

~

When breathing must slow

down and voice must lag,

the drum adds the chorus:

~

The snow covering mountains

dyes hair in cold wind.

~

Her voice wields a bamboo cane,
wears straw shoes for travel:

A reed mat will be my
house. Pine and bamboo trees

will be my walls.
Let's hang the moon

at the end of a drooping
cinnamon tree

~

She wishes to shine as the moon.

~

The pansori singer distills
her husband
from mulberry
leaves and lotus root, a drink

she spills from her mouth
while weeping.

~

This is her

grey hair song patient for
a food offering ritual at her

tomb: all worth less than
the wine
she drinks alive.

~

When the song is strong and loud,

the drum strikes the same—

the spirits feel their hearts.

Joseph Han

While Her Husband Wandered Southern Seoul

my grandmother stayed home. She met a begging
woman, a hidden boulder shaping spine into curve—

old age. *If you can sew, I will feed you for every
thread.* The beggar plucked the clouds and spun

reams of fabric, demanded a husband. *I cannot
provide what I no longer have.* The beggar's skin

crisped into leaves rotting without water. She brought
home a demon lover, outpouring demands.

Grandmother traced seams of clothes once
housing the sanctuary of flesh and love.

She cursed these spirits with every stitch,
tearing her fabric to blanket them. *These goblins*

*ferment in my home and breathe stench
on my sons.* Grandmother found a thread

on the floor, spooling from the garment in her
husband's coat. She held her line as the demons

scoffed against hope in his return, feeling tug
like earthquakes between her touch.

Marie Hara
Nekkid Secrets (1956–1958)

I heard the loud "Yooo-hooo!" that sounded like a lady calling out politely toward the house. This short girl started waving at me before I saw her on the other side of the fence. She was looking right at me. Bonnie ran out, handing over two sticky purple green mangoes. She spoke just to me. "You have your own radio?" Her large, bosomy mother, Mrs. Gant, looked out of their kitchen window as Bonnie and I talked story. We were both thirteen that summer. We smiled a lot. I was taller and skinnier than my classmates and admired Bonnie's soft shape and pleasant, easy-going ways. Everything about her was compact. Even her loafers had short pinkish tassel tips. I wanted to try them on, but I could wait. She said she listened to K-POI, my station, too. Not that I had my own portable transistor. I loved that she was *haole* with freckled skin and fine blowy hair like mine. Both of us had brown hair. I wondered, did she know I was *hapa*? We were pals. She was my friend, that's what mattered.

Meanwhile a lot had to get done while we moved in. After my mother and I dragged the 50-pound bag of rice through the kitchen door, we lugged it by the corners to O-Baban, seated on her bed, who pointed where to store it in the bedroom closet next to the stash of canned goods she kept her eye on. For once I had my own shelf and half of a closet for my collection of toys and special stuff. Mama patted me on the head and moved us out to the living room and the picture window. She raised the blinds and motioned to the street outside. "You see, this place get everything nice: school, bus line, small yard, and Auntie Ruth next door. Makiki, just right. Lucky, us." I liked her being happy for once while we swept out the floors and unpacked the boxes and bundles. I didn't even complain when I had to take out piles of old newspapers to the trash can.

Later I had to block out my mother's complaining about me

not helping clean the house that we now owned which was her dream come true. I noticed how cocky she was about passing her Practical Nurse exam and getting a new job at Tripler Army Medical Center. Mama kept talking about learning how to study so hard because she was serious about it. Now she was tired of watching me just read, lounging on the new Sears *koa* furniture. She claimed the tropical flower cushions were always getting messed. Mama wanted me to know that she had to work extra shifts to pay for the new place, which would be the start of so many things. She acted as if I wasn't doing my share or understanding the effort she was making for my sake, all the problems that came with responsibility, the word she threw in all the time. I was just happy that I could get away quickly to play with Bonnie as soon as Mama went rushing off to the hospital for her evening shift. O-Baban was so old, she didn't bother to tell on me, and next door Auntie Ruth just made a check mark on her calendar when she saw that I got home from school.

Since our mothers agreed that we could go over to each other's home, sometimes my buddy, that would be Bonnie, and I might take the green light to pretend that we were at each other's house when we walked far away together, to some spot like the coral bed at Ala Moana where they were building a brand new Liberty House. Or we might visit one of the Gant relatives' home in the Damon tract (called Chinese Hollywood) to peek around the fenced off H-1 before running back as if we had running practice going. We both tried to spot Chinese people, but they must have mostly stayed inside. Enjoying the freedom of doing something that we didn't have permission for, we moved unseen everywhere we could.

Bonnie showed me a place in the panax hedge between our houses where we could cut through noiselessly, instead of using the metal fence with a clicking gate latch. Bonnie watched me show off my talent using the Hula-Hoop. Then she did cartwheels all around the grass while I tried to copy her nonstop technique. We played marbles, checkers, jump rope, tetherball, all the box and board games we spotted, anything we could use to challenge each other. We competed on who was stronger and faked who could last longer, say in holding the breath. "Aaah, you chicken. Chicken bawk, bawk!" we called each other, when one of us began to lose speed or threatened to beat the other. When Bonnie yelled, "Chicken shet!" I countered, "Show-off!" back to her, and the contest restarted. If I won, she did next: we turned it over again. We added up points on all wins, including in time, every breaking of a chicken's wishbone to make something special come true. Believing in magic, we found a way to compete at singing, "When you wish upon a star, makes no difference who you are..." before the other one thought of doing it. The first with the song would then claim to win a future victory in spite of the other's annoyed complaints about the cheating action.

We even tried comparing parents. Bonnie always won on calling up her dad's reputation as a big beer drinker, since he could drink more beer than any one I might know. It was her way of saying my new dad didn't count in the measuring. I didn't want to mention Duffy's drinking at all. Since he didn't seem to be coming back from the mainland, I had to concede that there was no point in pushing this contest.

The most satisfying games were ways to hide in plain sight. In the beginning we checked out possibilities that lay all around us. Under the Gants' house were more closed off areas that held small unused household goods and dusty boxes. Very quietly, Bonnie entered their cluttered garage and opened the lock to a storage closet holding her brothers' wooden box of off-limits BB guns surrounded by all kinds of game equipment. We just looked around, taking in the mess, sizing up where we might hide. It was the boys who we needed to watch. They called us Dumb Clucks when they wanted to boss us. The three boys were noisy trouble, being competitive and excited about the chance to team up whenever they could. But we knew how to follow them around and suddenly disappear when they played their war games. Walking slowly, moving backwards and slipping away, reciting to each other, "Like fight? Go fight," we enjoyed our stealthy action.

Junior, the oldest who went to an all-boys high school, was forced by Mr. Gant to avoid any talk using *pidgin* or slang or even worse, *pidgin* slang. The younger two who attended English Standard public schools were younger than us and knew how to swear dirty, our group secret. The youngest was mostly silent.

We became choir members at Central Union Church, because Auntie Ruth got together with Mrs. Gant to deliver me to the Joyful Young Pilgrims Program. Bonnie and I practiced on late weekday afternoons with the gang in the small chapel and sang most Sundays. As faithful church members, Bonnie's parents and my aunt arrived at the church services and looked around for us at every choral activity. We knew we were being watched. I already had double duty having to attend Jodo Mission Temple classes, because of my grandma's wish to keep me Buddhist. Jesus and Buddha seemed to be on the adults' lips but not on my mind where the stories scrambled together. Still Bonnie tried to pronounce "Namandabutsu" and prodded me to say "Hallelujah, Amen" with a giggle.

The choir was the attraction to Bonnie and me. We kept it quiet. The boys we liked were the ones adults approved of, but those boys had secrets, too. As soon as the adults weren't watching, the guys might get rowdy or dance with their wild hip thrusting just barely staying out of notice. They sang pop songs and made up stupid lyrics. They could switch into hymns when a teacher walked in. They picked on the same few guys every time they could, pretending to hit or trip or push them. Sometimes they seemed to enjoy each other. Most were *haole,* others were Asian or part-Hawaiian or *hapa.* A lot of them went to Punahou or Roosevelt, only one to Washington Intermediate where I went. Bonnie was at the UH Lab School where she wanted to become a marching band baton twirler and didn't act like she noticed anyone, especially not the girls, but later on, everyone saw us as close pals.

Unknown to the others, she and I liked to call ourselves mezzo-sopranos, while the soloists who competed for roles were the coloraturas. We got a kick out of saying the fancy words that gave us a reason to laugh and point at each other while getting useless attention. The older solo girl singers acted as if they were humble about what they were chosen to sing, although they revealed emotions about their achievement after they performed. The guys were trying to sound like they had deep voices.

Together Bonnie and I listened silently to everything they sang or said, including all the gossip. We stayed aloof from the high jinks but enjoyed noting what we heard without adults around. During break time, the popular boys liked to brag that they snitched beer at home. Once outside of the building mostly all of them smoked, passing a cigarette around. We heard that when one well-liked boy wrapped his dad's Chevrolet around a tree taking a Tantalus curve too fast, he died in the wreck. It happened before we had joined choir. Everyone knew about it, although it wasn't to be talked about. That's how Fellowship worked. We looked for his face in the choir booklet photos and agreed that it was a pity he died. To us he was handsome.

Lots of us in the choir thought we could really sing. Maybe as a group we did, more or less, pretty much, with the exception of the lame ones who got away by just mouthing words. We had heard of the fame of groups like the Kingston Trio as well as all the pop stars that came to sing in Hawai'i. But what we trained for was a church production of *The Mikado*. The words were jarring to memorize, especially for the girls who had to sing "Three Little Maids are We, Tee-Hee-Hee." After the last show, we stood around for the curtain calls. Somehow we didn't laugh when Mr. Gant announced loudly that now we were "The famous Oriental Performing Stars" in his best sarcastic Ed Sullivan imitation. He was a boss at Pearl Harbor Shipyard and proud of singing lead parts in the Aloha Minstrels who were like a barbershop quartet, he said. Bonnie showed me his hat and cane, bow tie, vest, and pitch whistle when he wasn't home. Bonnie and I were never leads but always part of the chorus.

We loved to copy down lines from pop music magazines that printed lyrics to songs like "In the Still of the Night." When we got hooked, we listened constantly to Uncle Tom's Cabin broadcasts for all the top songs that we might hear, then hungered to get to the Civic Auditorium where we could scream, whoop, and swoon in pleasure to hear the new singers in person. A few years later Buddy

Holly, Paul Anka, Bobby Darin, then Elvis got us yelling for more. We listened to the high school guys talking about the lines of cars that circled Scotty's Drive-In then headed up to Tantalus where couples might go necking. They called it the Submarine Races. We babysat, watered yards, and mopped floors to earn the $2.50 for the tickets at the Civic Auditorium and talked about the girls who went with real dates and got in for free.

I took a black pen to scratch out my face in the school photos at the end of the year. During the summer Bonnie and I took photos of each other with her Brownie camera. We wore bathing suits and changed with each other to see how they looked even if we correctly predicted the black and white snapshots would be corny and needed to be hidden. I didn't want to wear my glasses and forgot to wear them whenever I remembered how I looked in the photos.

We sported our cute girl clothing and hair, the popular ponytails and stylish curled-under pageboys. Enthusiastic about looking older and fashionable we drew picture after picture of girls in profile wearing different colored skirts and blouses like the ones in the catalogs passed back and forth. Sharing a giant multicolored pencil set, we sharpened the lead carefully and vied for the brightest colors. We drew secret drawings of each other and squirreled away the results so that no one might see them. We wore girlish pastels and enormous crinolines under full skirts sometimes paired with white socks and loafers or sneakers. On a special day like Easter we wore fancy Day of the Week panties that no one would see but us. Bonnie still wore Mary Janes while I was faithful to wearing slippers or going *hadashi* as much as possible. Bonnie also had *haole* sandals. I longed for heeled shoes and pink pedal pushers to wear with a *palaka* shirt. As good girls, we plastered on only lip balm for shine then tried to bite our lips redder to look like we wore lipstick. Nestled in our palms, tiny eyeshadow sample sticks from someone whose mom was an Avon lady were secretly passed from hand to hand. Often we put on Hawaiian print *muʻu muʻu* and wore a plumeria blossom over one ear.

We knew all the good trees for different colored plumeria and argued over which ear the flower should be on. We could whip up *lei* in nothing flat. With a hug, we gave each other the *lei* we made.

We used words like "square," which we didn't want to be but suspected we were, pretty much. Knowing we were talked about, we didn't actually hear what was said or figure out who the kids meant. The neat boys had plain white T-shirts and jeans with jeans jackets. They did not talk to us. But right where we normally sat, one of them, we thought, left a Christmas card with B-O-N-N-I-E lettered on the envelope and no name signed inside, a mystery. We looked over all the boys but saw only what they wore. We overheard one say to another who looked like a rascal, "Eh, you wen spock um?" The rascal looked away from the prettiest high school girl, the one who was singing. He said, "Jes catchin' trills, brah." We had fun giving him the name Dopey and humming the Snow White marching song when we spotted him. But we preferred the ones who had some badness in them, the ones who did not see us at all. The tallest guy wore an old leather jacket that belonged to his brother who had been in the military. Sometimes the boys used beat up numbered athletic T-shirts or school jackets. Some wore aloha shirts that were super bright tucked into their khaki pants.

When I entered the Gant house, I heard that I didn't have to take off my slippers, not unusual, but there were other rules that I learned by heart. For a couple of intense years while I navigated a path through school, it was interesting to be where there was a father, a mother, my best friend and her siblings, even if they were quarrelsome boys. The Gants were my *haole* family. Using our whispered language, I backed Bonnie up when she dodged Junior, especially when Morris and Martin joined in, because they were too interested in mocking us. They tried to trap us in our words, then bark out laughs with their arms crossed at the ready to mimic what we said, how we said anything, and even what our expressions might reveal. Bonnie and I developed a secret hand and face code to pass signals of warning via motions for when to talk or hold silence. A casual hand gesture across my lips meant say nothing about whatever one of the boys brought up. I let their mom's instruction on how to be more polite and a better Christian bounce into my ears. It was like watching a tennis match when Mr. Gant commented on the comments. I knew that Mrs. Gant said pointed things to tame the boys, but I took the rules seriously. I had to learn how to set the table, to dab and pat a napkin on my lips, to drink my soup with the right spoon that went into the soup, then upwards to fill it with soup and then smoothly backwards into my mouth without spilling or choking. I got the part about how to butter only small portions of bread and how to be courteous in asking to have the dishes passed to me. I can't remember the sound of Mr. Gant's voice, but Mrs. Gant kept talking at the table to remind us that being well brought up and doing good things for others would show our inner worth. She also encouraged only pleasant conversation and modeled it for us. I noted that as long as I said please, thank you, and yes, ma'am in a soft voice, my pleasant conversation would be acceptable as good enough. I watched Bonnie doing it so well. Nothing to it. After a while no one spoke, and all eyes were turned elsewhere.

It was like the time I brought them a plate of shining slices of *sashimi* from my mother. Bonnie had tasted some before at our place, where she also poured *shoyu* directly on the bowlful of rice and didn't care when I said not to. No rice had been brought over with the fish, because Mama assumed everyone always had rice ready to eat. Mrs. Gant stopped Mr. Gant from making a chopsticks comment in the silence when I placed the platter down in the middle of the table. Bonnie scored points by being the only one to eat the raw fish with me. I thought it was a pity that there was no *shoyu* for the fish, but Bonnie made a show of licking her lips and saying yummy without catching her brothers' looks. But the other Gant family members didn't look right at me or eat the raw fish, although they all said thank you when dinner was over.

Bonnie's family was still way more lively than mine where the few words spoken were like, "You finish 'um up" or "Go clean da table." The Gant kids had the dishwashing job. In the kitchen, the boys did their best to hide actions bound to aggravate Bonnie and me. We retaliated by pointing at their stomachs and chanting, "Yum

yum, mum mum, tum tum." When little Martin brought in a bottle of their mom's "White Shoulders" perfume from the hiding place in Bonnie's room, he pretended to pour it in the sink. In turn, Morris stole it, holding it up high above our heads, beating our hands away. We played at jumping high to get it back, but when Junior came into the kitchen, he returned to his truculent self, giving us a hard look. "You stupid kids don't know a thing! This is from a man to a woman." He stormed off to report to his mother with the evidence of our wrongdoing. She punished us with a warning that we would not be making the special Betty Crocker cake mix for our strawberry shortcake if we girls couldn't be nicer to the boys.

I knew for myself I should never be nice to a boy. Even the word friend could not be attached to a boy in Mama's judgment. She would kill me if I even tried to be nice to one. When I found out from Bonnie that she had started her period, I took her to my bedroom closet where the enormous box of Kotex was neatly hidden behind my books. I showed Bonnie that I knew all about bulky cotton pads and the oversized elastic belt that needed to be positioned just right. We fingered the two metal hooks with jagged teeth that made the pad stay in place between the legs where it would continue to be unseen and unmentioned, a major secret trick for all females. Mama had told me all about pads, and gave me all kinds of advice about not ever getting pregnant, especially now that I knew all the reasons why it was important not to. It was all about eggs. I hoped Bonnie was impressed, but she just stared at the word Kotex, just like in the darkened school cafeteria where girls only sat together to stare at a special film that explained the scientific word "menstruation" using diagrams of our inner parts with eggs moving out and around. And blood, a mysterious source. Listening to Bonnie who talked so much about how her skirt hid everything underneath and then looked as if she had grown two inches taller because of her new status, I quickly turned the conversation to the bulky pads, could they be cut in half? She laughed at me, saying, "Don't worry, you'll get yours!" I didn't want to talk about how she was adult and knew the secrets. While I was left behind.

One humid Sunday when we didn't have to sing and no one would mention my absence at the temple, Bonnie and I went for a long hike through the pastures of Mānoa, up from Makiki where our houses lined the street next to the new freeway. The heavy air carried wet heat from slowly descending sheets of mist. We brought along Oreos, oranges, and a corked 7-Up bottle of water. Our plan was to head *mauka* toward the mountain range, past fenced horses and a few cows chewing on dry brown grass in their open grazing fields. We took turns carrying the paper bag of food. We passed Mānoa Housing and hiked up further, where we knew of turns on the stream and deep ponds we had been told to avoid, because they held the ghosts of drowned people like the one called *Obake* Pond. It wasn't one we would stop at, sort of too spooky.

The walk began to get hotter until we were slowing with the heat by the time we ate. But we kept at it. We knew the way to Mānoa Falls, a spot that promised us a small, heavy waterfall and not too hard climbing or too slippery mud that could make progress slower. Picking white and yellow ginger blossoms along the way we decorated each other with the cool, sweet scent drooping over our ears. We had thought we might go through the mist up higher on the welcoming green mountainside to another more secluded pond above the stream.

We sang songs loudly as we moved closer to the trail. We sang to drown each other out, "Blue Suede Shoes," "Tutti Frutti," and "Beyond the Reef," the fun ones that we sang over and over. We argued over changing the word girl to boy in "Dream Lover." We imitated deep voices, southern accents, and falsetto, too. When we reached a house in a clearing at the beginning of the path uphill, we heard part of a classical music recording, a silvery woman's voice answering a bold tenor's call, filling us with a new silence as we passed. The A-frame, wooden-shingled house looked like a fairy tale place. A small tethered goat baaah-ed while we moved through the softly filtered afternoon light. A golden butterfly flitted past us into the wide green field ahead.

I caught Bonnie unaware as she moved in and out of the

shadows beyond guava bushes and stalks of tall bamboo. She was thinking about something that made her frown when I got a clear look at a red-and-black-tailed bird making its soft movement high on a branch above her head. I saw her eyes dart up to the shrubbery. A small *'apapane* had appeared for a quick stop.

"Saw'm before you!" I guessed she would deny it.

"Nah, *I* saw'm way before you. Yay for me, *I'm* catchin' all good luck."

"So what kind bird? And no lie." She couldn't answer me. "Ha ha, I thought so! BAWK!"

"Whaat? What you said about me?" She tried to throw a dead-ripe guava at me and missed.

"*Liah, liah,* pants on *fiyah....*" I raced ahead of her.

We arrived nice and sticky from the length of the tromp through the pasture and the time it took to climb all the way into the forest, across the stream several times as we followed its bright, ready waters up and up. Passing the usual stop at the waterfall, we moved higher, following a white ribbon into the mountain. The quiet filled up with the trickling of water from afar. We rushed to the secluded pond, in a swoop to get toward the bracing water.

Bonnie carefully dipped her foot in the moving rivulets. She flicked me with sparkling drops.

"Well, I dare you go in the deep hole, little Miss Perfect, because you can't even swim like you say you can."

"So, so what? I double dare you follow me nekkid skinny-dipping, which you claim you hate, but you love so much. You *hana-koko-lele!*"

"Hoo hoo! *Shoots*...aah, cold, ooh!" Cold, the tingling relief against heat, was what we had chased all along. We dumped our old pants and limp shirts, our white panties, and only recently worn bras in a pile on the dry rocks. We had done it before and knew how. We crouched into the filled pool of coolness, enjoying every bit of wet comfort under the roar of the waterfall. Water reached our waists. We ducked in deeper at the same time and splashed each other without stop whenever we came up to gulp for breath.

As we played around for a while, we noticed bits of gravelly rock had been rolling down into the part of the pool where we swam. Raising our heads, we noticed dark silhouettes, two boys, clearly not adults, looking at us from the top of the waterfall about thirty feet above us. Curiously they said nothing and kept watching—one tall, moving, the other just standing. We went into the waterfall closer to the cavern's rock wall. While we crouched to hide ourselves, the water pelted down hitting the big boulders that looked like emerging umbrella shapes. The drops stopped for long moments before falling close to our bodies. I looked up to see if the watchers were still there, if they were still throwing gravel, but my angle was off so I was not able to make out who they were, whether boys we knew—what group? wearing familiar clothes? faces? *haole*? local? Wayne from Papakōlea? the guys who hung out with Harry S.? Velma's cousin? We asked each other quick questions without answers.

"Get out, look and see," I urged Bonnie.

"You go."

I stuck my head out of the waterfall, turning backward, looking up to the top of the falls where there was a flash of movement.

"Aaa...nooo, they still there."

Another dribble of small rocks confirmed it. "Let's go, get outta here..."

Bonnie looked like she was going to cry. "*Shet*! They gonna throw rocks at us if we move out."

"Not."

We had shriveled fingers and trembling blue lips when we looked at each other. We looked like we had drowned. Was this how the ones who drowned changed into *obake*?

Bonnie tried to get a look again and whispered, "I cannot see anybody. Oooh, I don't want them to see me all bare ass nekkid." She was shivering.

I looked upward through water, aware that if I moved out further in the small pool, the boys would be sizing up my body. It occurred to me so I said it. "Eh. They already saw."

Shame rushed over me from knowing I was baby pale and fattish, too. And I didn't want those guys to look me over and mark my hardly any *chi-chis*, my pink nipples like buttons. No thought of my now visible, crinkly crotch hair came to me when I crossed my arms across my chest in a scramble for the pile of clothes. Bonnie quickly followed me out.

There was only silence and water sounds. I looked back at the waterfall and the top of the cliff. No one stood up there. Nothing moved. I felt desperate to get away, but I had to get clothes on. Pulling on my increasingly wet underwear and jeans, I was spastic. My long hair whipped wet against my upper body. I turned myself in the direction we had come from, toward home, buttoning like crazy.

"Hurry, hurry...we have to...."

Our backs still to the cliff as we raced down the muddy path to the trail, we each looked again with distrust to see if we were still being spied on or being followed, to figure out what was next. Would they ambush us? Bonnie had her glasses on. She spotted something moving in the bushes at the top. She pointed at the cliff face higher up.

"What's happening? What are they doing now?"

We didn't know. As our footsteps slapped away on the path, we ached in the effort to run faster but not get hurt. Parents would ask questions.

"Don't say anything about this, okay?"

"No. *You* don't tell. Nobody."

We warned each other. Going down, unlike before, took forever. We compared the pain of the little cuts on our feet and fell silent.

After that day we talked grimly about each of the possible choirboys, the neighbor kids from our street, the friends of friends, even the newsboy, who couldn't have been there. *Who were they?* We listened intently to all the K-POI dedications. Would someone say something to make it like a joke?

We guessed about it day after day for a long time until we made it our top secret. But I really only wondered if the boys or one of them would call up Bonnie, not me. And would she ever tell me? She had the big *chi-chis*. I was the ugly one with a bad feeling, jealous of my best friend. I did not know how to fix it. For the first time I could not say anything to her about it.

Loneliness followed me.

Lisa Linn Kanae

Our Flying Circus

I remember,
my brother's worried face said
we must rescue it,
as he held the cassette in his cupped palm
as if the bramble of tape were a baby dove,
naked and blind.
To spool the cog, he
poked the sharpened pencil lead
between two tiny teeth and
rewound
the loppy
loop of loose tape
back up into
the cassette's plastic shell to
save sixty minutes of our
self-proclaimed comedic genius.

Our Flying Circus!!!
written in cursive across turquoise clouds
drawn on the cassette's label
before we recorded the opening line,
and now for something completely different, while
Mom served dinner rolls in Waikīkī where
insurance salesmen applauded a magician with pink,
feathery assistants beneath a mirror ball
spinning stars across a black ballroom.

Five miles mauka, we
sat in our Kapahulu apartment,
our faces lit shark belly blue

from the glow of the TV screen.
We sang along with the Monty Python crew about
lumberjacks wearing women's underwear and
"Lovely SPAM, Wonderful SPAM."

Mom baked SPAM like it was ham—
pineapple rings, brown sugar, cloves.
They eat SPAM too, we yelled.
Where is London, my brother asked?
Somewhere near California, I said.
They talk weird, my brother said.
Because they British, I said, like
Bond. James Bond, and if
they can write about SPAM…

Grab Mom's cassette player; check the battery.
Grab a Maxell; tear away the cellophane.
Grab my pen; grab your paper.
Press play and record—simultaneously.
You be Beanie; I'll be Cecil.
You be Gwasshoppah; I'll be the blind, all-seeing priest.
You be Cheech; I'll be Chong.
You be Jesus Christ Superstar; but I want to be
　　　　Jesus Christ Superstar.
You read *Mad*; I'll read *Mademoiselle.*
You smoke too much weed; I'll drop too many ludes.
You work at that gas station; I'll work at the mall.
You collect vinyl; I'll write love songs.
You be a good father; I'll be a college grad.
You get married; I'll get divorced.
You give a speech at my second wedding; I'll go
　　　　to your boy's Christmas recital.
You refuse another round of chemo.　　　　What will I do?

I remember,
My brother's worried face said
Our Flying Circus!!! was ruined.
The roles we played so well,
the conjuring of brilliant nonsense,
remains suspended in my memory,
like stars riding on that dark, dark wheel.

Lisa Linn Kanae

Two Groundbreaking Ceremonies at Lēʻahi

With this teaspoon of paʻakai wrapped in tī,
I close-off the difference between
the before and the present
to promise na kokolike
    —those who lived and died at the base of Lēʻahi Crater—
we will be vigilant. We will make this right.

We are a procession of forty,
each of us wrapped in kīhei made of
cloth the color of saline soil and
adorned with maile, tī, and kukui.
We carry ʻōʻō and bamboo stalks
filled with fresh water from Mānoa Valley.
The path we must walk is the path
nā kokolike still walks,
perhaps out of habit or love or grief.
We cross a parking lot, a cafeteria,
a Subway sandwich shop,
another parking lot, a bus stop.
I clutch my pillow of salt in my palm
as we step onto the base of Lēʻahi;
We know they—the spirits of this place—are
present among the overgrown weeds.

The procession stops five times—every fifty paces—to
chant to the five directions:
Hikina,
among the beer and soda cans
faded by sun after sun after sun.
Hema,

among the torn down, chain link fence
rusted by rain after rain after rain.
Komohana,
among the soggy mattresses,
the used condoms.
ʻĀkau,
among the grafitti spray-painted on Lēʻahi's face.
I Luna a I Lalo,
among our gods, and our Mother,
we are shocked by and ashamed of the
abuse and neglect.

Forgive us. Forgive us. Forgive us.

In the distance,
the faint sound of the pahu
calls us to walk toward the procession's end.
A rhythm rises from Lēʻahi and her ʻuhane,
a pace we are obligated to follow.
As the drum gets louder and louder,
we finally see the rented event tents
sheltering the mayor,
the administrators, the senators,
still holding iron shovels for
the public relations crew,
the television cameras,

but beneath the sun,
the pahu and its drummer,
the kumu and their students,
greet us, look into our eyes with
teary knowing.

From the five directions,
five students receive an ʻōʻō.

Standing before a dirt mound, they
pierce the land with their digging stick,
push into the soil a promise.
This will be a place of honor.
This will be a place of knowledge.
This will be a place of creativity.
Fresh water spills from bamboo stalks onto the mound.
He nuʻu hou o ko au ola.
This will be a place of new life.

Dawn Fraser Kawahara

The 6:54 am Rooster…

. . .announces
before the sun crawls up and over
to illumine your side of the rock pile mountain,
piercing the tangle of mango,
the dappled avenue of *kou* trees the County men planted
along the trail.

Your alarm, a postscript
as his tail feathers rustle, talons scrape damp grass
while seeking a fallen *noni* fruit,
lemon, tangerine.
His wary hens arrive with motley chicks—
peck-peck, jump at the bush of ripening chili peppers.
He heads the search toward the compost bin,
gulps lazy worms,
devours centipedes in fallen leaves,
they come upon the handful of rice,
the crumbled, stale saltines—peck-peck and gobble—
they fan across the lawn mowing their way to the borders,
the jungly no-man's-land.

Soon cock and harem exit the wire fence
choked with monstera vines,
leaving behind their hasty tracks.
That gang will be back by sundown
and then, again, next morning,
all will begin again.

The rooster's wake-up call,
late as it is, lingers. . .

You peck out lines, taste phrases, gobble words
at your desk all morning.
At noon you watch tropicbirds
wheel and swoop against the mountain,
birds like crumpled origami snatched from your waste bin,
ghosts of poem drafts floated by the wind.

How to spread folded wings,
launch out on the updrafts
realms above the path of shallow grub-and-find. . .

Jeffrey Thomas Leong
"No Dogs or Chinese Allowed"

Mythic sign in the Public Garden, Foreign Concessions, 1920s Shanghai, famously smashed by Bruce Lee in Fist of Fury *(1972).*

Capturing that mongrel pup
who laid tail about all the village routes, alleys, main streets,
to lick the boots, limped across a porch begging,
a pooch, to eat one day more.

In 1928, the Angel Island official interrogator repeats,
"Did you have one? A dog?"
Not the family pet but a mutt, secured on rice leavenings,
fahn jiu, scorched pot bottom and salt fish scraps,
a kind of canine garbage disposal.
Not man's bestie on its leash, a nightly stroll,
eater of nuggets in a bowl,
of oat gruel pressed into little wholes,
not that kind at all.

"Did you have a dog?" he insists,
as if an animal control officer, warden of the want,
decider of caged or uncaged,
who, or which, will meet their fate in the asking oven's perfect heat.
"Your alleged brother said *Yes*, but you said *No*. Then which is it?"
His pursuit designed to trip, exclude and restrict,
to push your lies to absurdity,
then out the Golden Gate, past Honolulu,
back into the old village.

Though now, you think, this is the one true
four-legged fact, though long in tooth

yet close to path
that you can relate honestly, kennel-free and without mewling.
Say, "Yes, now I remember…
when I left Siu Yuan village, we feasted
with my bound-feet grandmother who prepared a special treat
of snout and jaw, toes and paws, its last trot and waggle.
We leapt not wept, when she stir-fried then steamed…
of that house cur, no more.
We ate it."

Henry Wei Leung

Epithalamium

You weren't there, but I kept holding
polluted air in my palms to give to you
while our mother kneaded stacks of joss,
fanning them into fuel, and our aunts
unwrapped paper suits and paper shoes,
all tissue-thin, to dip into a bin of flames
for our long and recent dead that they
might dress to see your wedding day.

Eight thousand years, and our widows
still clutch this smoking loss for words
while your fingers pluck decay from old
kitchen leaves to keep the browning eyes
from the rest. We used to live in tenements
for the desiccated. We taped discarded
tarot cards to our rear bike wheels,
let them slap the rust from our spokes.

Will you still remember the tsunami watch?
I strained on a toilet on the third floor
while you and everyone climbed higher
to watch the flood that never came.
I washed in a bucket. That night we slept
on stranger carpet, our palms combing
the threaded nubs: pink in one direction,
maroon the other. Maroon the other—

Here is the one you've chosen.
He hurries us through airport crowds
and never looks back for you.

Corks pop free in a tongue of towers
beyond my learning. I learn how love
for home is always unrequited, and I steal,
just once, to remember you—when you
weren't there I stole one paper shoe.

Wing Tek Lum

Wedding Day

Her mother said by tradition she
should formally leave from our front door
for the ceremony. So she brings back
a bag with what she needs
to stay with us overnight.

Since her three uncles are sleeping
in her old room, she shares
the downstairs library with her aunt.
Cheekily, she suggests we close our bedroom
windows so she cannot hear our snores.

I wake up early as usual
going through my exercises, eating breakfast,
and showering. It is still dark;
the dawn must break
before anyone else stirs.

During the morning we work on our
last-minute cleaning since we will have
a lot of visitors, and a photographer
will be taking candids
around the house.

The coordinator drops off
the lei and flowers, coming in through
the back gate (which the yardmen
have left open).
I am startled by this.

Since I have some free time
I study the four-page printout
of the schedule
for the day. Everything is planned out
without much for my wife and me to do.

Near lunchtime I pick up for everyone
the sandwiches already on order;
I am the last to choose,
and eat one with ground beef,
which is surprisingly tasty.

After lunch a woman arrives to help
with hair and makeup. My wife's
turns out better than I thought it would,
her face, especially her forehead, for some
reason reminding me of a pearl.

She also makes up our daughter,
conservatively, with no heavy rouge
or lipstick, no black eyeliner
—though later on I overhear others ask
about her long false eyelashes.

Close classmates show up to help
with her dress. Although I brought it in,
this is the first time I see it out of its bag.
It is a strapless gown that reaches
to the ground. It looks just right on her.

The photographer takes pictures
of the girls and our family. Whenever
I am in the group, I try to lean in
or tilt my head towards the others;
but she keeps telling me I have to smile.

It takes me no time
to dress: my black pants, my white
long sleeve shirt, and my bright
red tie, which I brag to everyone
is the one I wore when we got married.

Our daughter leaves with her
classmates. I rented a van to carry my wife
and her siblings. As we get into our cars
the twins standing at their window
across the street wave to our procession.

At the park up on the mountain the couple
need to take more photos. My wife
especially likes it when he looks down
at the view while she approaches from behind,
and then he turns around for their first look.

Eventually everyone leaves to go to
the ceremony site, near a tree higher up.
My wife and I stay behind with our daughter,
so we can escort her. I take note of two
mosquito bites on her bare back, but say nothing.

Hidden from view, we have a far distance
to walk to the waiting guests. Everyone is
watching, making me nervous. When we
arrive she hugs each of us in turn. But I turn
the wrong way, and bump into her.

We stand to the side of the circle of guests,
not front and center. All I can see is her back
for the whole ceremony. I am
disappointed that we cannot see her face;
but I rationalize our guests can, which is good.

The officiant speaks
through her smartphone, which is hooked up
to a small speakerbox. They pass it
around so that each shares in their vows.
The words are soft, but earnest and clear.

After the ceremony, the groom's
father and I follow the newlyweds, talking
about how after so many years it is about time.
I utter the word "finally", making
sure both of them can hear.

All of us walk down to
the clearing for a group photo. Then we disperse,
in cars or in shuttle buses, to the restaurant,
to meet up again to celebrate what
we have witnessed, what they have done.

During cocktails, sushi is
served. As I mingle about, I notice
the young women helping at the reception table.
I bring each a plate of food
while we all wait for dinner to start.

Before the dinner my daughter dances
a hula in her long gown. The groom
however sits off to the side. I keep thinking
he will join in with her, but he just
watches: this dance is for him.

The lobster is nicely presented, but
when I cut into it, it seems
like my knife is too dull. Later on my wife
agrees that hers was overcooked too. It is too
bad; I want everything to be perfect.

I make it a point to stop at each table
of relatives and friends, to say at least a little
something to those I know.
This dinner is not for me, but still
I feel responsible.

At the tea pouring, I make loud slurps
exclaiming to everyone that this
is the most delicious drink I have ever
had. I raise my cup bottoms up
to show I have downed it all.

The dessert line has three
kinds of mochi ice cream. I want
to try each one, but worry
that they will run out. So
instead I take only two.

It is time to go, and we help by
taking home all their gifts. We say our
goodbyes to everyone. The new
wife and husband and their friends are
still dancing. Their night is young.

In the open courtyard I look up
at the sky, its air crisp after the storm
of the days before. The partial
moon, two-thirds obscured, beams a bright
crescent, a smile to share our joy.

Rajiv Mohabir

Aji's Song

We sat in Sonia-Pua's living room, some of my cousins sipping tea and others brandy. It was winter and the snow banks were taller than the car itself. Aji, my father's mother, had just recently cut her hair; her arms could no longer reach to comb it. It was so white, it sparkled blue and gold. She oiled her white tresses before twisting them into a bun that she piled on her head. Aji never wore her it down; it was a wild Guyanese bird.

Sonia-Pua's house was filled with laughter in English. My father, mother, sister, brother, and I loaded up the rental car and drove from Orlando to Toronto in a non-stop haze of coffee and calypso music blaring from the radio. It was Sonia-Pua's birthday and she was having a simple celebration—only inviting her siblings, which, including everyone, worked out to be twelve families plus Aji. I was the only one who called my grandmother Aji.

Aji's leaving Guyana was not of her own volition—she went where her children went. It was 1975, she had been widowed for ten years by the time her youngest made the motion to go to school in Toronto. Her other children: her sons and daughters already left Guyana in pursuit of fortune to London and New York. The four: Aji, Sonia-Pua, Rani-Pua, and Pua went to visit Toronto on tourist visas and overstayed. Pua married to stay in Canada and then sponsored Aji to move herself. Because Sonia-Pua and Rani-Pua were minors they were allowed to stay too.

Aji acquiesced and left her mango and coconut trees, the hourie and gilbakka sea, the parrots and twa-twa birds in the sky, the black trenches filled with hassa-fish to grow bora and tomatoes on a concrete balcony in a Scarborough tenement. Aji left the Mahrajin, the pandit's wife, the milkman, her brothers and sisters, her parosi, her neighbors, the colorful village gossip. She was caged here in an endless winter, friendless except for the Jamaican woman down the hall who had her own concerns. No one in the market was able to speak to Aji; she knew no "proper" English, was illiterate, and also called her Hindustani "broken." And that's how people treated her, like she was broken. When she arrived in Toronto her children told her not to speak her broken *languages in public. "You must say CAAAAAAR, not CYAAAR," one uncle used to say. It was better if she didn't do anything to embarrass them.*

Aji sat on the floor in Sonia-Pua's living room. She wasn't entirely able to follow her children's and her grandchildren's fast English. Never did she light on the couch. Rather, she hunched over her plate of daal, rice, and bhaji on the floor and ate with her fingers. I sat next to her, chatting while she gnawed whole wiri-wiri peppers like candy.

This woman who has come so far lives in a place where she is like a bird with clipped wings, I thought. How is she able to never fully communicate with anyone because no one speaks all of her languages? Being so isolated in this hostile and racist place must be difficult for her—those stares from people in her building, the sideways glances from white Canadians upset that she is benefiting from the welfare system, her children who ignore her during their get-togethers. She must feel like Sita, exiled from her own home, again. What does it mean to be completely dependent on a system that thinks you're an idiot?

"But Aji, Ram bura hai, Sita ke ban mein chhordawe khatir, na? Wasn't Ram bad for what he did to Sita?" I asked her in Guyanese Bhojpuri. She used to love to tell the story of the Ramayana and I loved to listen. Ram abandoned Sita in the forest after she faithfully followed him into exile for fourteen years instead of living like a princess. This was done when she was pregnant. It's kind of like Aji being widowed at the age of forty-four, I thought—to fend for herself and her thirteen children alone in Berbice.

"Yes, he was, beta. What men do in this world is awful. But what can a woman do?" she asked.

"Well, Sita eventually told Ram that when he abandoned her

in the forest that she was pregnant with Luv and Kus and then asked Mother Earth to swallow her whole." I piped up.

"True true thing, beta, what Ram do no one else go do. He exile he pregnant wife." She looked out of the window at the snow, which had begun to fall again. The flakes scraped the windowpane with their crystalline bodies. Some in clumps of twenty. Some solitary yet ornate.

Silence. My mouth burned.

We sat looking outside at the snowfall for several minutes. "Ekgo gaana sikhawa, na, Ajiya?" I asked, "Teach me one song, na, Aji?"

Just then my cousin Steven walked in and sat next to me on the couch. Steven was ten years younger and had lived in Toronto his entire life.

Aji unfolded a song of separation and the loneliness of betrayal:

Akhiya hamar badal rukhi
kahi naahi sukhi sukhi
tinhu lok me hamesa
tohar birha se hi bhigal

Sare duniya me ghumat hai
pavan aur nadi ka pani se
ekgo hi nisan paye ke
baras me kehar aram karab
hamar saiya baahar bhejaile.

"What does that mean?" Steven asked, narrowing his eyes. I was the only one in the house that could speak Aji's three languages. Our parents all started taking communion and going by their "Christian names" for the sake of assimilation or genuine faith. It must be genuine faith when the only way to get an education was to go to the Lutheran school. It must be genuine faith when the only way to get scholarships was to mimic the British and look down on the *coolie* parts of yourself. To survive you had to create social distance between yourself and the other crab-dogs by claiming an air of superiority through mimicry. Some of that superiority meant not learning your mother's songs, calling daal *split pea soup*, calling aloo *potatoes*, calling yourself James when your name was *Janghbahadur*.

I spent many days like this, sitting and listening to Aji's songs. I translated the best I could,

> *My eyes are clouds*
> *nowhere is dry.*
> *The three worlds are forever*
> *soaked in grief.*
>
> *I roam the earth*
> *for signs in*
> *wind and river.*
> *When rain falls will I stay dry*
> *my love has exiled me.*

"So Sita is in the forest?" he looked around. He was raised Christian and was taught to shun anything and everything Hindu. Just then Rani-Pua, Steven's mother, walked past. She must have heard us say the name "Sita" because she poked her red hair into the room.

"What are you talking about?" her smile was acerbic and stung.

"Nothing—me na know what kine madness dis one a talk," Aji replied before I could answer. She didn't want to upset her daughter. Aji's survival strategy: diminish yourself for the wants and needs of your children who want to assimilate.

"You mean, 'I don't know why he's asking these sorts of questions,'" correcting her mother's English. Her voice was almost British lilt as she glowered at me as if to say: "Don't fill my son's head with your Hindu nonsense." She had come a long, long way from where she had once been.

There was one market where she was able to talk to the shopkeeper, it was called PD Market, though she called it Pirri's *after the proprietor. He would greet her "Ram Ram, Nani" when she walked in.*

"Tohar jiew achcha hai?" she would respond. As a child I loved this dance between them. It was the only time when I felt Aji was joyful, when she was reminded of home.

They conversed entirely in Hindi: the shop owner speaking Western Standard Hindi and Aji speaking Guyanese Bhopuri. After greeting the dukanwallah we walked to the back of the store where Pirri's parrot perched. She would say "Ram Ram" and the bird would call out "Ram Ram" in reply. It was a blue and gold macaw, the same kind that she had had when she was a little girl living in New Amsterdam.

It was time to cut the cake. Pua called us all into the kitchen where she lit the ten candles on the cake. It was white. White as refined sugar. White as snow. White as English. Sonia-Pua blew out the small yellow flames that flickered and died releasing their last breaths of smoke: white and curly. Outside winter kept brushing its feathers against the doors and windows.

Everyone: my cousins, aunts, uncles, mother, father, brother, and sister took the white cake in deep into their intestines. We were warm inside drinking tea and sugaring ourselves. We ate cake and licked the frosting from plates and forks. We laughed and painted our lips in white frosting. We curled our tongues around the frills, the letters on the cake that read "Happy Birthday Edith." Edith was Sonia-Pua's "Christian name." We spoke fast English with correct grammar, my Canadian cousins with the proper "Eh's" and us Floridians with the requisite "y'all's." It was a blizzard of ascendancy. My father and his siblings must have thought, "We no longer lived in the village and only dreamt of eating cake. This was our own cake."

Aji was eating her daughter's "Christian name" in the next room when I came in and sat next to her. She ate with her hands.

"Raimie! Come!" I could hear Sonia-Pua calling for me from her couch. It was time for us all to sing. Usually during these events, Will-Phupha brings his guitar and everyone assembled sings old calypso songs. "You can't leave until you sing us all a Hindi song," Sonia-Pua said half-genuinely and half-testing me to see if I actually knew any.

Rabaht, Aji's mother's macaw was completely wild and would visit their house for leftover rice and daal in the morning. Her mother would call, "Rabaht, Rabaht, Aao, khana khao." And Rabaht's blue and gold feathers would appear. Aji held the rice and peanuts in her hand while Rabaht perched on the fence in front of the house and ate from her open hands.

They kept feeding it and it would follow Aji to the market where she would buy more peanuts to feed him. He even knew a couple words and phrases like "Sita-Ram" and "Betiya" which was what Aji's mother called her. They were friends, about the same age. Rabaht had just showed up one day and Aji's mother had fed him. When he came back the next day Aji's mother fed him again. When the third day came when Rabaht ate from her hands, the family adopted him. There was no need to cage Rabaht or to clip his wings. He lived outside, wild, and came and went as he pleased.

One day Aji's mother went outside with her plate as usual and called for Rabaht. She called for hours but Rabaht never came. She left the plate outside until the rice dried up, uneaten by the parrot but scavenged by ants. Rabaht never returned after that. She suspected that the bird had been caught and sold to the United States as an exotic pet, or taken and killed for its feathers.

Pirri's was the only parrot in Aji's Toronto, in the familiar smells of the Indian market, but askew, as it was not quite her own: Indian but not Guyanese Indian. "India-man different kine people," she used to say. Their language, their Hinduism, their songs.

I sat on the crushed velvet couch and wiped the sweat off my palms on my jeans. The afternoon sun was now looking into the window where I sat, my aunts and uncles encircling me. There was silence. What song should I play? Everyone wants to hear something that they know, or something that's current. Maybe I should play

"Mere Sapno Ki Rani" or "Suhani Raat"? These were crowd pleasers. All of my Puas sat forward in their chairs. I thought of Aji and how she was listening from the floor of the next room. What song would she want to hear? I started to pick the chords, A minor, G, A minor, G. I caught the rhythm began,

Akhiya hamar badal rukhi
kahi naahi sukhi sukhi
tinhu lok me hamesa
tohar birha se hi bhigal…

Aji unfolded her legs and rose. She walked in her empire-waist floral print frock and shuffled into the room where we all sat in her music. She sat on the couch next to me. She sat on the couch and continued singing with me,

Sare duniya me ghumat hai
pavan aur nadi ka pani se
ekgo hi nisan paye ke
baras me kehar aram karab
hamar saiya baahar bhejaile.

Tears glinted like Sita's golden deer in my Puas' eyes. They sat mouths gaping. How did Ma know this song that Raimie is singing? Maybe she saw it on a Hindi film, but that's impossible, Ma only knows *broken* Hindi, I imagined they thought. Finally Sonia-Pua spoke, "How does Ma know this song?" I was right. They were amazed that their mother knew such a beautiful song. She shook her head in disbelief.

"This is Aji's song, not mine." I answered gesturing with my head at Aji who now shared this crushed velvet with me.

"Me mummah been sing dis song come time fe plant rice," Aji said. It's a work song, a song that women sang from the rice fields, that Aji and I sang now from a middle-class living room in Brampton, Ontario. I thought of all the women who sang this song once. How it was important for both the work but also in expressing sadness of leaving their father's homes, for leaving their India to come away to Guyana, and now, how Aji sang this song of bitter separation having left her home for the snow.

Sonia-Pua began, "Wow, you're a real Indian Cat Stevens." It was her way of diminishing Aji and me, jealous that her own children didn't know Aji the way that I did.

If she was being derisive or mean it didn't matter. Aji was perched on the couch next to me growing back her tropical plume.

Shareen K. Murayama

A Loincloth, a Necklace of Whale's Tooth, and a War Club

I. Days of Defilement

The mountain stream silenced the chanting of ʻAkahiakuleana.
Its arms cupped her from the night's blackness.
Her stream breathed softer with each moon's sitting.

The water stepped to the falls' steady dance.
ʻAkahiakuleana walked and slept in the pond
until her skin became soft like the surface
and slick like the leaves at its bottom.
The water cradled her and the sun and moon, five times over.

It was on ʻAkahiakuleana's final bathing day that Līloa of Waipiʻo—
Līloa, father of Hākau, Līloa, husband of Piena—
saw ʻAkahiakuleana in the Hoea Stream.
He saw her nakedness and beauty.
His hunger rose until he, she, and the stream moved together,
and their son ʻUmi was conceived.

II. ʻAkahiakuleana and Returning Home

With Līloa's war club in her hand
and his lei niho palaoa cradled in his loincloth,
ʻAkahiakuleana turned her back on the flowing river.
The valley's wind blew her hair
with the shadows of his touch,
the smell of his skin lost beneath the horizon and the sun.

Alone she began her upward climb,
the weight of Līloa still pressing against her:
a growing seed, and hope for her child's future.
Many sharp rocks covered her pathway.

III. The Child Is Not Yours That You Should Beat Him

ʻAkahiakuleana watched her husband's frustrations with ʻUmi
grow wild and plentiful from within
as if her husband's bones whispered to his heart:
This son is not your son.

Tired of his father's beating,
ʻUmi's own bones whispered to his heart
an answer he already knew.
ʻUmi asked, "Have I not a different father?"

ʻAkahiakuleana sat down with the truth:
the shooting ferns, the rushing water, and
Līloa's loincloth wading in the stream.

ʻAkahiakuleana was a descendant of royal blood. Chief Līloa, ruler of the island of Hawaiʻi approximately 400 years before Kamehameha I, was taken by her beauty and lived with her for a short time as he journeyed through his lands near Hilo. Both were married to other partners when they met.

Andrew Najberg

1st Island Fisherman Mending his Nets

When I lie flat   on the dock
Over Raci Cove

And look down the slats

They stretch   infinitely
Into the sky

Water heard but not seen

I graze my cheek   on gritty planks
And listen

To boisterous screams of girls leaping

From the posts   into the foamy
Current eddies

Wood rattle as the fisherman

Drops his lobster   traps
To dingy boat bottom

He doesn't know when he wafts

His net for one last   check
of the twine

That he's casting to catch

the solar flares
in his weaving

Earlier that day I saw him

Smoking hand rolled cigarettes
On his porch

While he plucked the net strings

Like playing a guitar
Lips pressed tight

He hummed the melody

His hands did not make
Who knew

How ambitious his song.

Lark Omura
Prison Street Mangoes

When Great-grandpa died, he left behind
an aged plantation house, eight mango trees heavy with fruit
in its yard, and a concrete slab of patio where four generations
learned to tread carefully the powdery red dirt
of his acre on Prison Street.

Back then, summer meant cramming into Dad's blue pickup
taking the ocean road across the island to pick fruit
before it began to fall. My siblings and I were spotters
shrieking out warm-colored clusters amid feathery green.
Our father maneuvered the net on his bamboo picker
straight to them, then sent it our way, bulging.
We ushered the prizes into five-gallon buckets
growing heavy as the day grew hotter.

Too many not to share, cardboard soda boxes lined with newspaper
and fruit were dropped at the names on Grandma's list
then brought to classrooms, neighbors, and the owners
of our favorite Thai restaurant, who'd send us home
            with a spicy feast.

"Best mango I've ever had in my life!"
My father would slice them in half against the seed
crisscross his blade through a bowl of orange flesh
and push the skin inside out, popping out rows
            of perfectly cubed bites
sticky juice making veins down his dark wrists.

Those Prison Street mangoes are supreme to all.
Sweeter in the heat of the tropics, sweat and nectar
blend down chin and neck bite by bite.
You'll never want one anywhere else.
Today, I walk the aisles of my grocery and glaze
right over them, small green fruit in wooden crates.
Even their skin seems duller, no shiny sap staining it
like when picked straight from the tree.

Recently my sister sent me a picture
from Grandpa's old house, the yard the morning after a storm.
Rust-colored earth a still-drying damp shade of brown.
Mangoes were everywhere—so many they blocked
the walking path, brilliant rocks scattered over ground
dried leaves curled around them.
A red plastic rake leaned against a tree in the shade.
I saved the photo, so when people ask what it's like there
I can show them. Mangoes, the best you'll ever eat
as far as the eye can see. Red and green and amber
jewels sitting freely upon earth.
And my young sister, her fresh womanhood
invisible behind the lens of the camera
probably laughing at a joke with my father.
I can see them now: she in shorts with legs the color of cream
and coffee, he bent over on the wooden stool
a thin gray cat whispering figure eights
at his heels.

Shandhini Raidoo

Deliquescence

I know a girl
Who has lived in the same house since birth,
Who is afraid to move ten minutes
away to her grandmother's. She's made
This island a whole world. If I tell her
What it is to be fluid
She might not thrive. Survive even. Become
Clear and unseen, like the act of dissolving in water.
Except in Majuro, which is becoming macabre.
There is nowhere to go, especially for the dead
when the water comes. Instead children
Are left to play among the headstones
Leaning in the wet sand after the dollhouses
are washed away. Where else, ancestors,
When the lagoon and the Pacific
Dissolve the atoll? Perhaps Pohnpei
Is becoming more like Pompeii every day,
Minus the romance. There is no one left
To displace, with grace or not. And what
will you do with your mothers?

Shandhini Raidoo

Liliko'i

Condensed milk is so sweet
It can cut your teeth, but they're only milk themselves,
And the crunch of seeds like sand
is bitter in your mouth. You're not supposed to bite,
but it's better than a mango, and purple.

Every continent is an island too,
But islands aren't allowed
to be continents themselves. It doesn't matter
Your skin—like favored fruit, in every language
another name, an other self
Sweet and sour, slippery and hard.

Synonymous with sweat, with skin
With the start of everything: fresh juice
needs only an introduction from an errant seed.
There are only so many words, you think,
For a home that you carry
like a turtle on the inside.

In the market, sweat courses down like rivulets
The body you have run. Yellow-green
Knocking hollow like knees: if something
Familiar is here, in among the frangipani,
It's still America after all, unexpected itself.

Salt

Kalihi Gate, Symbol of Progress

The funk was the big old chain with the lock
Holding the gate closed across the road by the
NO TRESPASSING sign.
We'd just walk around the old gate under the avocado tree.
It's not really the end of the road either.
The road goes on up past the water tank,
Colorful with graffiti partly painted over.
But now the gate looks like the water co.'s
Brought in a small prison and stacked it,
Chain links and spirals of barbed wire
By the masseur's house at the back of Kalihi.
I guess they don't want us hiking up there,
Falling down their cliffs, no our cliffs,
Swimming in the waterfalls.
And it was partly our fault.
The Saturday before our boy was to graduate from Farrington
We climbed up there and down the cliff to the falls
With a nurse's family from Michigan
And a minister and her husband from Transylvania
And Lucky Dog.
We'd finished our cold water, lung-gasping swim,
And were pulling ourselves up the rope, feet dug into the crumbly
soil,
When Mike decided Lucky Dog, all scrambling around,
Was bothering me. He left the rope to chase after the dog.
Only his face with a helpless expression on the front of his head
On his sliding down body, hands grasping at stringy bushes
Whose roots came loose too, came shooting by me.
And I wasn't quick enough or strong enough to grab him.
Avoiding the next climbers he came to a thumping halt

At the bottom of the eroded gully.
"Are you all right?" "No,"
And the nurse tossed me his phone.
Faster than thought, I pulled myself to the top and dialed 911.
I knew I was in trouble too when the voice asked me my number,
And I didn't know it. Maybe that's how they test for shock.
But I knew where we were.
In minutes a helicopter circled us.
Next two police cars, a fire engine and an ambulance
Pulled over on Likelike. I didn't think about the afternoon traffic,
But friends told me later they were stuck in our mess for hours.
The helicopter and the firemen seemed to play a verbal tug of war
To decide who'd get Mike out, but soon it was six firemen
Carrying an erector set sled who used me as a landmark to find him.
They passed him up like a bucket of water being shunted along to a
fire.
Wet in my bathing suit, I trailed them back to the ambulance
And drove to Queens with them.
Still if that happens to someone even just once a year,
Those waterfall swims are worth it all. The water co. just doesn't
understand.
Besides we'll get around the barbed wire.

Normie Salvador

Breaking Isolation

Beneath the room number is a plaque:
"Isolation."
I hesitate at the open doorway.

Because this morning I woke still hacking,
we pause at the overhead
supply cabinets and sink.
With practiced ease, my sister pulls
down a box and passes to me
a paper mask. Before accepting,
I ahem and clear my throat.

We pause at the second door.
My sister glances at me and pauses,
"It's backwards… and upside down."
She watches me re-apply the mask:
crimping the embedded metal strip
across the bridge of my nose,
tugging crisp accordion folds over my chin.

With a nod, she unlatches the door.
Our parents look up: our mother from her armchair,
our father from the hospital bed.
As I see my father for the first time
in a week, I cough.

John E. Simonds

Troubled Hands

The back of my hand held me hostage last summer
while something wild turned it
swollen and black,
then red and brown,
advancing as an alien,
purpling the fingers,
hatching its own flesh
in a "Birth of Adam" wake-up
morphing left-hand skin.
First an emerging turtle shell,
then a thick burnt biscuit
cobbled upward to a leather nest
set in a crater of darkened hand.
Sinews, veins, and nervy parts
hiding under an eschar dome
drew life and strength from
green-gray forearm, elbow to shoulder,
but, as predicted, the creature peaked,
evolving to a muffin scab,
easing apart from bleeding edges,
like a crust lifting off a red-fruit tart,
surface near-perfect round and changing,
to a stew of yellow-green tissue,
exposed like a motley pie of tendons and tendrils,
to be washed and bandaged each night
in a nerve-center circle from wrist to knuckles.

In autumn therapy at Hale Pawaʻa
others with problem hands reach out
for treatment to restore their use.

The husky young man in horizontal stripes
was hard to ignore, but we worked at doing so.
I did my best to focus on the machine
where flying bits of corn husk pelted
my hand in a chamber of swirling hot air.
I stole glances at him and his guarding men,
badges glinting on their bulgy shirts.
Later, heated towels sandwiched my tape-bent fingers
crunching them closer to palm.
Then we dipped the hand in liquid paraffin,
a hot wax treatment pinched in towels.
The man in stripes left soon with his keepers,
we others busy with our eyes and hands,
maybe wondering, as I did, what had hurt
an inmate's hand to warrant outside treatment.
Was it survival, escape, a machine-shop wound
or one of those stoic "falls"
prison life seems to accept
with close-mouthed grace.
He was one who knew what hurt him,
one of thousands in island prisons,
lucky not to be boarding at one
of our privatized mainland Guantanamos
and to live when felons no longer
forfeit hands to penal butchers.
My hand is more a mystery to me
than his condition likely is to him,
mine a broken blood vessel
worsened by blood-thinner pills,
waking at 3:30 a.m. in swelling pain,
building to a special effects blood cluster.

With no driving, life became
a schedule for TheBus.
Heat wave minutes passed like hours

in the path of kitchen exhaust,
shattered only by hurricane warnings
announced on TV with buzzer alerts—
deep electric sounds like prison door signals
as gates are opened and closed one day to the next.
We learned TheBus, overcame oxycodone,
got lucky with hurricanes, kept arms and elbows
nerve-cooled with icy bundles of frozen peas,
a vegetable diet that left us 10 pounds lighter
when the soupy wound closed near Hallowe'en.

Each visit to Hale Pawaʻa brings hope the striped man
will show, his treatment a signal reminder
that lives are often a series of visits,
too short, or with no end in sight,
like pain that arrives before dawn
and stays until we survive or escape it.
We need to signal the man to support
his recovery, hoping our fingers can close
to flash him the greeting sign.

Helen Sina

Bonesongs

ʻŌʻū—*ʻōʻō* already lost. *ʻApapane*—
ʻelepaio disappearing. Their songs
rise up from bones to fall as wind
feathers on the curve of air. Cascades
of crystal spill around us—ghosts
of bonesongs wanting to be heard.

Music is born in the bones
of singers with names like songs.
Once their music filled the air—
called up morning—crowded the
day with alarm—the music of mating.
Echoed the comforts of shelter.

Imagine all the bones of all
the birds no longer flying this small
island. Layers of lost *iwi* waiting
for their songs to soar the sky.

Joseph Stanton

Sandalwood

Hiking the Waiʻanaes, we're surprised
to see a sandalwood tree,
ancient remnant
miraculously in bloom, high

in mountain air
secured by roots—
insidious, parasitic—
adhering to an obscure crag.

Blossoming bright red,
it drops remembrances
of trails past
where long-ago men—

bent question marks—
stumbled, bleeding,
under aromatic burdens
of broken heartwood,

bringing down
to the greedy kings and merchants
the sweet, precious (now forgotten)
fragrance.

Joseph Stanton

Wilderness Management

The ʻalalā, the Hawaiian crow,
is endangered,
that we know,
but we also know the ʻio,
the Hawaiian hawk,

endangered also,
eats the ʻalalā as fast
as the birders release
the captive-hatched crows
back into the wild.

This hardly seems sporting.
The breeders should,
at the very least,
import endangered eagles
to eat the hawks.

Bill Teter
Stepping Twice into the Same River

"I'm just one of those people," she said, leaning confidentially toward me, as if we were a secret cabal of some sort, "who hate when anything changes."

It was very early. We were alone in the laundromat, me with my thoughts and a stack of student papers to grade, her with her whole world in tied-up plastic bags hanging over the edges of her Longs shopping cart. She had already borrowed several dollars in quarters from me and shown me how dirty her blouse was. "Look at all that. It came from my hair. I hate when my hair is dirty."

Outside a heavy Mānoa rain was making it hard on the folks setting up the Sunday morning farmers' market. I had a long day ahead of me, and it was too early for my head to be churning like it was. On the radio when I woke up this morning, a man was listing all the familiar landmarks of his childhood that had disappeared: the pay phone; dial-up Internet (with that weird, sci-fi-sounding beeping and buzzing as the computer sought connection); encyclopedias. "Everything now is Googled or Binged or stashed on little micro thingies or up in the clouds," he complained.

I had been thinking of this since I turned the radio off and got out of bed, thinking too of the sounds I had not heard in years: the busy signal; or those first few seconds of popping silence when the needle first came down on the vinyl record; or *I love you. I'm so glad you're in my life.* A moment ago, I had been staring at the glass face of the washing machine, and the face reflected back to me, unmoving, superimposed on a background of rolling and tumbling clothes—I tried hard to believe it was mine.

The shopping cart lady appeared across the folding table from me, blocking my view of my reflection. "Did you know they tore down the Sears at Ala Moana? It's gone—just gone. I don't like that." She shook her head emphatically and looked over the bags on her cart. "Remember when Ala Moana had Liberty House? Then it was Macy's. And Byron's out at the airport is gone, too. They just tore it down." A pause. "I don't like that either." She had spoken softly, but her voice was rising with intensity now. "It's a tragedy," she continued. "I went looking for McDonald's on Ke'eaumoku. I couldn't find it."

I said, "It's still there. They just fixed it up."

"Everything is changed," she said. "I don't like change. I don't like it at all." She fumbled in one of her bags and fingered out an opened package of crackers. She put one in her mouth and began to chew. She mumbled, "And Don Quijote Restaurant is gone. And now Holiday Mart is Don Quijote—but a different one." She paused. To catch her breath? To find the right words? "It's very hard," she said. "I cannot handle."

I nodded. *Yes, it can be hard*, I thought. *Change is everything. As Heraclitus said, you cannot step twice into the same river.*

"I'm Tanya," she said. "What's your name?" I told her it was Peter, and I wondered why I lied. There was a time when I would have given my name without hesitation. When did *that* change happen? And why?

She was silent. As I watched her nervously untie and retie her bags, I thought about what she had said, and a parade of changes came to me. Arakawa's was gone. The 'Ewa sugar mill was gone. There was no more TGIF beer and barbeque in the courtyard of the Hawai'i Institute of Geophysics—or if there was, it wasn't like it had been when I was at UH. What else? Varsity Theatre—gone. My life with Lynn. Gone.

I tried to shake off the feeling. I didn't believe all change is bad. I didn't want to be thinking like Tanya. I knew it was a cliché (not to mention inaccurate) to dwell on the past, to remember everything as having been better back then, when there was less traffic, when life seemed slower, when I had less stomach and more hair. When I was in Lynn's life and she was in mine.

Tanya was getting to me. Her hair was dirty and matted. Her several layers of clothing needed washing more than the rags she'd put in the machine. Her eyes were fearful. Too much change. Too much that was lost, too much that was different. Too much out of place, or gone, or replaced by something inferior. Too much, all of it, too much to handle.

I was starting to feel that way myself. Too much change, I was starting to believe, and none of it good. Itchy, looking for something to do with my hands, I unfolded the towels I had already pulled from the dryer and folded them again. When did I become who I was now? When did that change happen? I didn't want that change. I liked the person I was before I became who I was now. Was that change why Lynn was gone? Or had her leaving led to the change?

Self-pity. Another change. When did I start feeling sorry for myself like this? It was almost enough to make me hate Tanya and her shopping cart life. She was finished with her bags now and was staring at me, squinting, reading my face. She opened her mouth to speak, then changed her mind. Her face went blank and she wheeled her cart around, heading towards the door and a Mānoa morning still drenched in gray rain. "I'll be back in a while," she called over her shoulder. Then she stopped at the door. "You know, Peter," she said, "they tore down the KFC across Ala Moana. It's a tragedy. I don't like when things change."

And then she was gone.

And I turned back to my changed, unhappy face in the glass of the washing machine, a world of clothes tumbling and spinning behind it.

That evening I watched the sea and the sunset from Diamond Head Road. Below me, afternoon surfers drifted on the waters, thin lines of surf advancing toward them. The sun dropped below overhanging clouds and glazed the ocean surface gold. The waves rolled toward the shore, blue to gold to white. A low soft rumble came up to me from the surf below. Over my head, the clouds shaded from white toward orange. The waves rolled, the surfers floated, the sun eased down into the west—the whole world darkening, slowly, beautifully, as it does every day, as it has done—unchangingly—always.

Laurie Scott Tomchak

Bus Stop

Monday

Arriving in the rain at the bus stop only to find the covered bus stop bench totally occupied by a homeless woman sleeping. Joined another rider hunched under a shop awning.

Tuesday

A knight of woeful countenance says to me that his eyesight is too weak to read the number of the approaching bus. I looked where he was pointing and saw no bus. All I can tell him was that there is only one bus that stops at this bus stop, and it is the 56 bus, and therefore by definition it is the right bus.

When the bus came, he was still sitting on the bench and not moving towards the boarding area a little further on. "The bus is coming," I told him. He cupped his hand around his ear and I repeated my words. It's sad when our senses desert us.

Wednesday

Trapped at the bus stop with two women talking VERY LOUD. They are both grandmas at 37. They get along better with men than with women. Their daughters are VERY STRONG WOMEN. More like men than women. So they get along with them. One woman is getting over problems with drugs, the other with alcohol. I tried to tune them out, but my hearing problem had magically disappeared. I probably would have liked them in another context. The bus didn't come for another half hour. It seemed longer.

Thursday

Early this morning a woman is talking loudly on the phone to her son. The grandma is dying of cancer, and they're going to Skype with her. The lady sitting next to me is scanning her phone and muttering, "You're talking so loud." The mutterer asks me, "Is the next one going to be a 57?" I make non-committal noises in the form of 57 bus anecdotes. An older woman says to the mutterer: "What a beautiful sunrise! Do you see it where you live?" The lady says venomously, "No, I leave the house too early to see it. I work six days a week and I don't feel like talking. Sorry to be rude, but please don't talk to me." We all lean way from the angry one.

Friday

At a night bus stop, a woman asks me. "Does the six stop here?" I say that it does, and right after that a car with three other people comes and picks her up. Does she just have an idle curiosity about buses? A boy asks me, "Does the six stop here?" I say it does, and he walks away. Are there people who avoid the six bus like the proverbial plague? I mean, it's not entirely reliable, but it's by no means the worst thing in the world.

Saturday

I run for a six bus and miss it. Meditating sadly on the expression, "she missed the bus." Have I missed the bus? At least I haven't been thrown under the bus.

THE BUS GOES

Monday

The eerie feeling that your reading material is altering the universe. As I read a memoir by Grayson Perry, a trans ceramic artist, three trans people get on board. One had a beard and a mini-skirt, one a dress and black lace tights, one hot pants, a tank top, and a long red ponytail. I'd only seen the bearded one before. This time he is eating red Twizzlers.

Tuesday

A fellow is talking loudly on the phone and is saying that he is going downtown to collect three debts. It's not like he's a loan shark or anything: he doesn't charge interest. When the person on the other end of the line asks him how he's going to do that, he says, "I've got my ways." To another question, he replies, "No, I'm not going to beat him up. That's how I ended up in jail the other time." When he is about to deplane, I notice that he is wearing two hats, a baseball cap and a fedora, one on top of the other.

Wednesday

A man gets on the bus in his wheelchair laughing uproariously and conducting an orchestra with one hand, watching himself in the bus window. He looks around at all of us as if to say, "Isn't this fun?"

Thursday

A guy gets on the bus carrying two soggy paper bags of stuff. I remember I have a paper bag with reinforced handles in my pack, so I get it out. A young girl in back of me asks if I want her to take it to the fellow. When she does, a guy sitting nearby helps him transfer the stuff. I feel like am in a happy Broadway musical. (Only takes a few minutes of work to cut me back down to size).

Friday

A guy gets on the bus carrying a Chihuahua wearing a comfort animal harness. He is a lightly bearded worried man who obviously needs comfort. A lady in front of me begins fawning over the poor animal, which also looks worried. She tries to get the man to sit down by me so she can continue fawning. He moves away, and the dog relaxes, looking relieved.

Saturday

A cat is on the bus! He has a harness! He is gray and white with tabbyish patches!

Sunday

A woman sits with one of her running shoes untied. A fellow sitting across from her with a can points it at the offending foot and says, "Your shoe's untied." She ignores him, stares straight ahead. The guy sitting next to her says, "I tried to tell her." As she gets off the bus, the driver tells her that her shoe is untied. No reaction.

After she is gone, one of the guys says, "We tried to tell her." This gave way to a drama where the guy with the cane waved it in the air and almost put out someone's eye.

Monday

The witching hour on the bus begins at dark. A graybeard (his long beard and hair are a little bit yellowish) sits on one of the forward facing seats with his head bent forward in the aisle and his head down. At one point in the ride, he gets up and stands in front of a man who is sitting in an elderly and disabled seat. He bends over and seems to be whispering to him. The other man ignores him. A stern lady sitting nearby tells the graybeard to go back to his seat. He obeys. Another lady covers her face with a towel to avoid his fragrance.

Tuesday

A man in a wheelchair is secured with the belts called "securements." A woman boards with a gigantic walker, filled with mysterious objects in clear plastic sacks (foil wrapped food? empty jars?). Now no one can enter through the front door. At first, the woman gets out each time the bus stops and gets back on afterwards, dragging her walker. Then the poor driver devises the solution of taking the new passengers to the side door and specially letting them in. Each group of passengers takes a while to catch on to what is expected of them. The walker woman keeps up a running commentary, like a sports announcer. The wheelchair man is silent.

THE BUS GOES CRAZY

Between two stops on the Kailua-bound 56, the digital display changes to 1/1/00. I look around and don't see anything that couldn't have been present on that millennial date. Were we briefly time travelling, or was the bus experiencing nostalgia? I looked around and everyone is sleeping. Twilight Zone music, please.

Joseph Tsujimoto

Plan B

Often, our banter is a kind of contest; either of us, usually myself, will say, I'm going to pass before you do, and she'll shake her head in protest and say, No, I will. And childishly I will say, I said it first, and then she will recount her hospital record, which I will counter with mine, however feeble my list, though equal to hers in extremity, if not in frequency, as the nurse appears, like Lady Macbeth, from a dark doorway, ticking off names of patients to be weighed, measured, interrogated, ready to go, my parking voucher already stamped, as I hold my breath while we descend the elevator smelling of contagion; no ghost, but absence, in the machine. *I* will, I say. The clinic is open 24/7. Our house is just beyond the first bend in the road, beneath the blinking street lamp. Like the flashing light of the ambulance, we're used to the noise and the buzzing.

Lance Uyeda
School Violence

1. Incident Report

_Theft x Assault _Accident _Vandalism _Trespasser
_Unauthorized Access _Motor Vehicle Accident _Hazard
_Unauthorized Use _Sexual Assault _Unauthorized Access
_Suspicious Behavior _Other:

Description of Incident:

The girl with blood on her face screams at her friend. The friend, unmoving, silent, looks as though she's wondering how to turn the girl inside out. A red ribbon, starting from the girl's nose, runs down her chin and onto her shirt. (cont'd)

Suspect Description:

Sex: F Age: 25 Height: 5'6" Weight: 180 Build: husky
Hair: black Hat:_ Glasses:_ Scars/Tattoos:_
Shirt: white tank top Pants/Skirt: black jeans
Shoes: white sneakers Other clothing:_ Weapons? Y
Type (describe): car
Vehicle description: white late 90s Ford Taurus

Description of Incident, cont'd:

"You fuckin' punched me, Olive," screams Blood Ribbon, who can't have done nothing to her baleful friend. Olive steps forward as if to indulge her punching preferences yet again, but now I'm here, and so is Serena, the counselor.

We've come upon the scene from different directions. I was headed to the cafeteria. Serena was going to a class to guest speak on the meaning of satisfactory academic progress, or something. I'm useless, but she's calm and knows what to do.

"Let's try to talk about what's happening," Serena says to everyone. I suppose talking is an option. I wouldn't say that I'm ready to make my getaway, necessarily.

Olive's large, white car is running. It looks like a police cruiser, more than fast enough if you don't care what it bangs. She has driven down a small lane between buildings that has no parking, so it's possible that she's brought Blood Ribbon to the doorstep of her classroom. But something has changed her desire to make friendly gestures. She hasn't turned off her engine, but has chased the girl out the passenger side. Blood Ribbon, between probably ill-considered pronouncements that Olive is going to get it now, reveals that more than safety or escape, she wants her property.

"Gimme my bag," she says.

I wonder if all this is because someone tried to kiss someone else. Their problem, whatever it is, seems solvable. If only I had a magic wand, I could make these people disappear and go on my merry way. Serena calls 911.

"The police are coming," she says. (cont'd)

2. Incident Report

_Theft x Assault _Accident _Vandalism _Trespasser
_Unauthorized Access _Motor Vehicle Accident _Hazard
_Unauthorized Use _Sexual Assault _Unauthorized Access
_Suspicious Behavior x Other: MMAction

Description of Incident:

In my classroom are two boys who've somehow become locked together on the floor in the manner of snakes at sexy time. If this were happening elsewhere, in a porno, for instance, or another class, it might be hot. But even now, thinking of them there gives me a shameful jolt. One second, I'm teaching college. The next, I'm pining for a giant leg of Grandma's to hide behind. "Jesus," I want to say, "at least take your shirts off first," but instead, I peep, "Hey, stop!" (cont'd)

Suspect Description:
Sex: M Age: 18 Height: 5'8" Weight: 160 Build: athletic
Hair: brown Hat:_ Glasses:_ Scars/Tattoos:_
Shirt: gray Pants/Skirt: black shorts
Shoes: slippers Other clothing:_ Weapons? human body
Type (describe): huggable
Vehicle description:________________________

Suspect Description:
Sex: M Age: 18 Height: 5'7" Weight: 150 Build: athletic
Hair: black Hat:_ Glasses:_ Scars/Tattoos: yes
Shirt: black Pants/Skirt: black shorts Shoes: slippers
Other clothing:_ Weapons? experience and training
Type (describe): thug life
Vehicle description:________________________

Description of Incident, cont'd:

In my class, a packed conference room because why not, there's chair inequality. Some chairs have arms and cushioned seats and sit around a conference table. Others are third grade classroom chair-desks, pushed back against the wall.

I make them get up and rearrange themselves for group work often. By now they should be used to it. I like to use the time they take to find and form their groups to write notes or instructions on the board. I have to turn my back to them to do so.

Step 1: Share your answers to the question with your group. Step 2: Discuss...

"That's my fucking chair," Marker BJ says.

"Fuck you," says St. George Pierre.

Later, my colleagues will ask whether there had been anything brewing between them, and I'll say no. They both just happen to be the kind of young man who harbors a special talent, what you see in your quiet friend when she has two drinks and begins to order songs at the karaoke bar, only instead of singing, it's falling down and hugging people in such as way that their ability to punch, choke, or kick is neutralized.

Before the floor-based hugging, though, there are preliminaries, such as heavy breathing, a face-off, and the grabbing of shirts. These take five seconds, or ten. I'm getting an education in what the steps to fighting are. Once each has the other's shirt in hand, there's no turning back.

"Hey, hey!" I say, repeatedly.

I think it's Marker BJ who body slams St. George Pierre, but it could be the other way around. I'm concerned for the person being slammed, of course, but I also worry about the wall and chairs. The faculty senate meets in this room. Luckily, the room's unscathed, and the boys' long embrace starts immediately. The bottom boy puts the top one in a mixed martial arts leg hug. Or perhaps each leg is a free agent. They're both nice and strong. (cont'd)

3. Incident Report

_Theft _Assault _Accident _Vandalism _Trespasser
_Unauthorized Access _Motor Vehicle Accident _Hazard
_Unauthorized Use _Sexual Assault _Unauthorized Access
_Suspicious Behavior _x_Other: Verbal altercation

Description of Incident:

The woman who in a year or two will have been pressed by gravity and life into a psychotic slouch, and who will announce to a new class that gay rights are a form of mass hysteria, is playing teacher. Next year, she'll say that we ought to be mindful of the uses of stoning, which was how in the past the community took care of homosexuals. This morning, she's taken it upon herself to help her two teammates, one of whom has a higher grade than she does, to learn vocabulary words, which is not what we're doing. We're in another cramped room, a converted study space in the library basement, in which I'm attempting group work. Neither have I learned.

Across the room is the girl who can squint disgustedly at everything on Earth while never looking up. I need—when I worry whether she might, through excessive phone homing and eye rolling, give herself a seizure—to tell myself no, that's not possible. She more closely resembles condensed formaldehyde than the gem for which she's named, so let's call her Bakelite.

Suspect Description:
Sex: F Age: 60 Height: 5'6" Weight: 170 Build: husky
Hair: blond Hat:_ Glasses:_ Scars/Tattoos:_
Shirt: black sparkly blouse Pants/Skirt: blue jeans
Shoes: black sandals Other clothing:_ Weapons?_
Type (describe):______________________________
Vehicle description:__________________________

Suspect Description:
Sex: F Age: 18 Height: 5'9" Weight: 150 Build: slender
Hair: black Hat:_ Glasses:_ Scars/Tattoos:_
Shirt: blue Pants/Skirt: white shorts Shoes: pink sneakers Other clothing:_ Weapons?_
Type (describe):______________________________
Vehicle description:__________________________

Description of Incident, cont'd:

All semester long there has been an asymmetrical cold war between Homophoba and the woman Lila, from the Czech Republic, who sounds urbane and European when she speaks, which is often, and who on more than one occasion has told the class about her experiences working as a dolphin trainer in Indonesia. Although close to Homophoba in age, she has worked recently as a dolphin trainer, and it is not difficult to imagine her in a faraway land being catapulted by dolphins into complex aerial maneuvers.

Homophoba, for her part, has repeatedly brought us cookies from Safeway, despite the signs that forbid eating in the classroom and my no-cookies reminders. Today Lila is absent, so it's her turn to be the star.

Bakelite loves Lila. She doesn't look at or speak with her too often, but when she does, it's with a smile that cracks her forlorn mask.

This is the second semester she and Lila have been in the same English class. They've come to me as a group, she and Lila, with the Marshallese lay pastor Isaac, and with Jamaal from Somalia, who speaks softly and aims for employment in the state sheriff division. Homophoba looks at them and sees that they have had months of bonding without her.

It must be something for Bakelite to see Homophoba, excluded from the invisible circle to which she herself belongs, still racked with hope that her life will change. What is she, Bakelite, in her child's ponytail, if not under the shoes of everyone she's ever known? The smelly feet. Who make her tend to the horde of their offspring, and take her goddamned camping.

With each passing year, she gains another handhold on her own life. Someday, the ones above her will step aside, finally, or die.

Homophoba has not been one to stand clear, or get ahead. At the board, giving dubious advice to her team about the word "milieu," she utters what Bakelite hears as Lila's name.

Why Bakelite says anything about anything is a mystery, but here an utterance comes. Her head tilts upward. Her eyes cast side to side at first, so infrequently are they used to look into the middle distance. They land finally on what could be her grandmother prancing about, begging everyone for attention, when the rule is that grandmothers should sit in stillness and wait for the world to come to them. Perhaps Homophoba is an affront to nature. Perhaps she's terrifying.

"Don't talk about Lila when she's not here," says Bakelite, almost yelling.

"Don't you raise your voice at me," says Homophoba. "I didn't say her name." She adds, "But I can say anyone's name I like: Lila, Lila, Lila!"

Some mornings Homophoba comes to class needing to

anatomize a verbal trouncing she's received from someone—her ex, maybe, or one of her children. "What's a narcissist?" she asks.

Despite how badly she loses to whomever it is who calls her names, she's a match for Bakelite. "Lila, Lila, Lila!" she says, wagging her finger.

"Why don't you sit down and shut up!" screams Bakelite, standing.

"Don't you mess with me!" yells Homophoba, eyes on fire inside her skull.

"Okay, okay," I say, my hands in the air.

One of them screams about the long-term impacts this exchange will have on the other's future. One of them engages now in an aggressive hoot series of vocalizations but will later slouch, whine, and cry in the vice chancellor's office to escape all consequences. One of them is supposed to be seeing the school's mental health counselor and has said she sometimes feels like using a sharp implement to make incisions in people. One of them will never apologize.

They continue to scream and scream. I wish, I don't know, a social worker were here. For occasions such as this. In a blue uniform, with very large blankets. A uniformed social worker carrying 1) a flashlight, 2) a mallet with which to tap lightly on knee caps, and 3) a clipboard. All in blue, she listens and tries to figure out what happened. She stops the screaming, of course, with her social work strategies and personal charisma. There is no taking of the screaming down the hall or into the library.

4. Other

Years ago, a young woman, Patience, wrote her first college paper on the time she was punched in the face by her guy, which made her tooth fly out. She picked it up and paid for her own dentist visits.

A middle-aged mother, Houdinae, told me in my office that to get to school, she'd packed a bag and made a budget. Then she'd planned day-by-day, week-by-week, and month-by-month to escape with her daughter from her boyfriend's apartment. She was lucky, she explained, that she'd had a job. They want to control you, she said.

Lexa, in recovery from crystal meth, stood up in class and shared that Truman Capote's *In Cold Blood* reminded her of her brother. I let my daughters stay with him, she said. He raped them.

Constance, as a teenager, had been sold to a pimp by her dad. Now that her dad was old, she was spending time with him again.

There was a woman, Honora, who once sat with me and said that she'd had a heart attack, and so had her husband. And then he'd tried to kill himself, and she'd tried to kill herself. And her husband's sister had, during the time the two of them were in the hospital for heart attacks and attempted suicides, died in a car crash in California. The sister's spouse died. Their children died, too. And without asking her what she wanted, but suspecting she regretted signing up for my class, I promised to give her an "N" grade, which was better than an F because it would preserve her GPA. I gestured toward the box of Kleenex I had on my desk for crying students even though she wasn't crying. Maybe it was all true.

5. Incident Report, cont'd

_Theft _x_Assault _Accident _Vandalism _Trespasser
_Unauthorized Access _Motor Vehicle Accident _Hazard
_Unauthorized Use _Sexual Assault _Unauthorized Access
_Suspicious Behavior _x_Other: MMAction

Description of Incident, cont'd:

What a blessing it is, really, that both these young men can fight; they're not just full of shit! How much worse things could have been if in the course of the heavy breathing and shirt-pulling run-up to the main event there had been a miscalculation. There might have been some eye gouging or nut kicking then.

A middle-aged woman, Maryland, who pulls eight- or nine-hour night shifts at a care home and comes to class straight from work, catches my eye and asks if she should go for help. Yes, go for help, I tell her, not meaning that she should run outside yelling, "Help!"

Marker BJ and St. George Pierre both have friends in the class, another stroke of luck, and these friends stand by, encouraging them to let each other go. Maryland must have alerted every other instructor in the building by now, but none has come.

It's okay, though. Each has a bro at his side. The bro code is strong. They release one another.

Not long from now, as the centerpiece of the Psi Beta domestic violence awareness fair, there will be a campus march. We'll print signs, tape them to sticks, and cheer. The march will trace a circle on the Great Lawn. At the head of the parade will be a golf cart with balloons tied to it.

This is what St. George and Marker BJ need: not fans or viewers, not an audience, but engaged, polite protesters. What young man doesn't need at one time or another to be encircled by a ragtag train of golf cart followers chanting, "Shatter the silence, stop the violence"?

When they hear that security is on its way, St. George seems appropriately chastened and adopts a posture of waiting, but Marker BJ understands the situation differently.

"I better not get in trouble for this," he says. He also mutters, "I should'a licked him."

The realization dawning on him is that he's in a place where his recent exploits might be interpreted as something other than a display of skill and mercy. He exclaims more forcefully now, "I'm not getting in trouble for this." Even if his speech patterns haven't developed much in the thirteen years since he was five, the sentiments we all express at that age aren't necessarily un-adult. He leaves at a trot, declaring again that he will have no trouble.

When Marker BJ is outside, he circles back to the classroom window and hocks a loogie on it. Sitting on the pane of glass amidst flecks of dust and grime, his loogie's like a mucus flower, stretching its roots for water.

6. Incident Report, cont'd

_Theft x Assault _Accident _Vandalism _Trespasser
_Unauthorized Access _Motor Vehicle Accident _Hazard
_Unauthorized Use _Sexual Assault _Unauthorized Access
_Suspicious Behavior _Other:

Description of Incident, cont'd:

Olive makes a mental calculation. She wants to punch her friend again, but there's little time. Her car's still running. She gets in and throws the girl's bag out the window, onto the ground.

Blood Ribbon doesn't go for it. She stands in front of the car instead. She doesn't seem to realize that there are durable social advantages to being hit in public but not hitting back. All she sees is that the tide has turned in her favor.

I'd say what she wants is a public takedown of Olive, a scene from tagalong-with-the-cops reality TV. Olive might, she imagines, cry. She might protest her innocence. Perhaps instead of supplication, she'll offer the police a theory on weather-related nosebleeds. It's so hot today, she'll explain, trying to dissociate her fist from Blood Ribbon's condition. Anything can happen.

Blood Ribbon lowers herself into a goalie's crouch. Behind her, she intuits, is Olive's freedom.

The car jerks forward. Before it, the girl is even thinner and more birdlike than before. She takes a step back, but the step is a small one, and she keeps her hands out in front of her.

"You're not going to get away, Olive!" she screams, her eyes locked on her adversary.

Olive pumps the brakes again. She grips the wheel and glowers out from behind the glass. As if swatting at a fly, she waves at Blood Ribbon to move. She seems annoyed at having to make such a gesture. Even when not lurching forward erratically, her car has the scampering out of its way of pedestrians as a feature.

Questions to which the answers are probably yes:

Is Olive also an aggrieved party? Did Blood Ribbon hit her first? Is it Olive's fault that, when hit, the girl turned out to have dainty veins?

Description of Incident, cont'd:

In front of Blood Ribbon is an expansive, white car hood. In Hawai'i, every child learns to dive into blue or green water and not to bellyflop on sand. So it could be that this girl grew up elsewhere, or that she has seen one or fifty too many movies in which a person on a car, not in it, ends up fine.

Somehow I miss her leap. She must've used a half-running start. A fender makes a good foothold. The next thing I know, she's sprawled atop the car, and from where I'm standing, I can see her face. She looks pleased with herself.

Her eyes widen with fear when Olive lurches forward again, gassing it a bit this time and then jerking still. Olive screams at her to get off the car. Her screamed reply reiterates that Olive isn't going anywhere. She's spread-eagled on the hood.

Olive pushes the gas pedal down. They're all definitely going somewhere now, Blood Ribbon on the car and Olive in it. My ideas about safe speeds of travel are changed by seeing them rocket down the lane to the main road and off to the cafeteria. Olive isn't hungry because they ate lunch earlier. When Olive takes a sharp left turn to head toward the campus exit, Blood Ribbon is still holding on. That's the last we see of them.

Note:

Later, when the campus director of safety and security calls to ask for my account of this occasion, he'll tell me that Blood Ribbon has returned to the state hospital, where she's a psychiatric patient. He won't say what happened to Olive. I'll tell him that I was there. He'll have to calculate my uselessness.

Description of Incident, concluded:

For now, Blood Ribbon is on a ride. If Olive were a better driver, or less angry, Blood Ribbon could climb onto the roof and car surf, howling. Or turn somersaults, chirping like a dolphin. Lila tells me that dolphins, already amazing creatures, if trained properly are effective therapy animals.

To protect herself in case of a fall, Blood Ribbon covers herself in scarves, wrapping them tightly around her arms and legs. Each time she ties on a scarf, a piece of her body disappearing behind it, she says aloud a demeaning or abusive thing. She has hundreds of scarves in her pockets for this kind of situation. Then she's supposed to take off the scarves one by one and say *I'm beautiful, I'm loved*, and other affirmative sentences, but she tends to lose scarves this way.

It's good to escape. Serena walks down to the office to say what she's seen, but I'm late to lunch.

Julia Wieting
‘Ohana House

The light enters differently
in our ‘ohana house
now darker after
slapdash attached
to the new complex, the big
front house meant to muscle out
termite ridden affordable history
from a newly concrete Kaimukī
of runoff and desert.

The name for this now
what is it portico
veranda lanai dogtrot
overhang fixed hinge
gangplank bridge
breezeway awning
cover roof attached to
new electric meter box.
5/8” plywood, too few joists
shingle nailed and boards
tacked on to reduce
the sheer

(sheer is sideways pull).

We came home and the lot
was pick-up-sticksed
into a pile of splinters.
The sky was blue
and the dirt was brown dried
Diamond Head ichor.

The caterpillar's assistant
irrigated the dust
and there was room
now clearing
now enough light to change
the hose's surge into rainbow
sheen.
Now is painted concrete brick
now is suddenly
something four apartments
and two garage
studios.

The good days are quiet
and the bad days quietly
test the insulating factor
of overhead doors.

This new territory
separates the false kin
of tenants. We anchor
tolerance of each other
to this shadow over
dusty ground and
lean into the now.

BAMBOO SHOOTS

Selections from our online writing community.

Doreen E. Beyer

Those were the days, my friend…

Dad removes the fresh mochi from the mochi maker and slices it to near perfect squares for the ozoni that mom makes only at New Year's. A memory breathes of a time when Japanese ceremonial tradition demanded pounding the mochi by hand—fathers lifting and dropping the heavy *kine*, resembling a giant mallet, into the sticky mound of undifferentiated rice; mothers risking a hand to shift and move the rice for evenness. The pounding finds a rhythm and a harmonic counterpart is perfected. In the back patio, the mochi maker sits with calm indifference to earlier whispers of rice spirits.

Jim Harstad

Old Slim

He held his left lat with his big right hand and doubled over, gasping with laughter, struggling to keep the fruit jar in his left hand from spilling.

Old Slim Remington finished a full gallon of Petri fortified white and watched TV evangelists every night of the year. Bought us beer and never took a cut.

Old Slim'd done some boxing.

"Slim," we'd say, "heard you had the champ worried."

"Yeah. Third round. Thought he'd killed me. Wha, whee, wheeze."

After high school, I moved to Seattle. My mom sent me the obit:

Remington, Leonard. Retsil groundskeeper, age 36. Stroke.

Scott K. Kikkawa

Riesling Goes with Anything

She knew everything.

At least she always sounded like she did.

"Riesling goes with anything," she proclaimed with authority. Those proclamations always came before an audience of more than me. After a few weeks with her I was beyond impressing.

"Anything?" gasped one of her vapid coworkers, the one who crocheted those doll torso toilet paper covers for office craft fairs. "Really?"

"Sure," she replied. Big smug, Estée Lauder grin. "With anything on this table."

Right.

Even with the fucking shoyu chicken.

They all lined up for a pour.

Not me.

I'd seen this show.

I reached for the scotch.

Bill Teter

Falling Sky

Some days on the road that fall I felt like we were all kidnap victims, my father some desperate outlaw trying to get us as far away from the scene of the crime as quickly as he could. Other days I felt like we were all fugitives on the run. Most of the time, though, I felt like we were being drawn west toward some terrible future. Though my father's hands were on the steering wheel he was not in control. We were going to live in California, and he was going to war. At night in my journal I practiced writing the word "Afghanistan."

We had Thanksgiving dinner at a Sizzler Restaurant in Tucumcari, New Mexico. My little sister Marla whimpered that there was no cranberry sauce. Mother spoke softly to her. My father stabbed his steak like it was an enemy.

My parents argued every day, beginning in the darkness of the motel rooms before we kids were awake. I slept in a sleeping bag on the floor, Marla on an extra cot if the motel had one, in bed with Mom and Dad if not. In the dark, pretending to be asleep, I'd roll onto my back so I could listen with both ears. I couldn't hear much other than their urgent voices, and I didn't dare open my eyes. Even now whenever I think of their fights that fall I cannot conjure up any visual memories—just disembodied voices whispering in the blackness, like co-conspirators.

This was the daily routine: Dad with his heavy foot, apparently eager to get to California, to be gone, and Mom finding various ways to slow him down, almost dragging her feet on the road. His foot on the gas, hers somehow on the brake. And so we staggered west.

Kristel Yoneda

Hook

The thrill and possibility of a first date.

"I don't do small talk," she grins, a flirtatious challenge to bookend our evening.

I'm still nursing my second drink, the glass sweating in my hand. "Isn't this how you get to know someone?"

"You'll ask about my job or if I have pets, but what do you learn about me other than adjectives? Just say something true about yourself."

I unfasten my watch to reveal a crooked scar on my wrist. She traces her index finger along my childhood casualty like a treasure map, hooking herself to the space between my skin and shirt sleeve, pulling our orbits together.

SPECIAL PREVIEW

What We Must Remember

The next issue of *Bamboo Ridge* (#111) will be a new collection by the award-winning authors of *No Choice but to Follow* (*BR* #96), Christy Passion, Ann Inoshita, Juliet S. Kono, and Jean Yamasaki Toyama. *What We Must Remember* will feature 28 linked poems, followed by insightful commentary on each poem by its author. With an introduction and timeline of events by Massie scholar John P. Rosa, this special issue revisits the 1932 kidnapping and murder of Native Hawaiian prize fighter Joseph Kahahawai and the events surrounding it, commonly known as "The Massie Affair."

Referred to as "one of the greatest criminal cases of modern times" by the *Chicago Tribune*, the incident was reflective of the racial tensions in plantation-era Hawai'i and, according to scholar David Stannard in his book *Honor Killing*, "provided the seedbed for subsequent [social] change" in the local community. In this new book, each poet investigates, interrogates, and brings to light the racial, ethical, and moral complexities of one of Hawai'i's most controversial criminal cases, the linked verses interwoven with factual detail to create a mosaic of emotional depth that explores the implications of the historical events that took place and that continue to reverberate today.

We are pleased to share the following excerpts from *What We Must Remember*.

Christy Passion

Reading Assignment: Stannard's *Honor Killing*

I don't want to read this story.

Don't want to know their names, imagine their faces.

I catch my breath as the words surface:
Tin Can Alley, barefeet football,
brown-skinned boys wearing white silk shirts.
See them behind the wheel—immortal for the night;
hear the ease in their laughter
stronger than daylight and the poor.

Too close to home.

It is my father's stories of his Hawai'i.
There were few comforts, but
there were dances at the Ala Wai Club,
Violet's in Kalihi—stew bowl for 25 cents,
there were beatings, Japs, Haoles, Blahlaz, and curfew;
dirty cops way too willing, rats that climbed up
tin gutters, girls with nice legs who gave it up
easy, and if you were lucky, real lucky,
a job at the shipyard.

Was different back den Chris
no can believe, was so hard. But we work,
go drink, talk story, forget for little while

This is not Michener's Hawai'i.

I skip to the end where she commits suicide—
and like a child burning ants, feel
a false sense of power. The end gathers me up
for the journey back.

This story is the unwanted family heirloom
the ugly vase,
the chipped china,
the bastard child everyone whispers about,
but no one calls by name.

Ann Inoshita

One Call: Sunday, September 13, 1931

Saturday night wasn't busy in the Kapiʻolani building,
so no one from the Honolulu police could predict
an early morning phone call
that changed Hawaiʻi forever.

Before the call came, Agnes Peeples
walked into the building at 12:45 a.m.
Agnes said her husband was driving
when they encountered a car filled with men
where King and Liliha intersect.

Although the cars didn't hit,
Agnes and a man from the other car fought,
resulting in blood seeping from her ear.
She remembered the car's license number: 58-985,
and Officer Cecil Rickard recorded her statement.

The phone rings at 1:47 a.m.,
so Captain Hans Kashiwabara picks up.
Tommie Massie reports an assault
and wants the police to visit his house.

The captain calls Detective John Jardine.
Then Jardine contacts Rickard
who instructs police to drive to the Massie home.

Detective Harbottle, Detective Furtado, and Officer Simerson
listen as Thalia Massie speaks:

She was at the Ala Wai Inn
and went for a walk at about midnight
when a car with four or five Hawaiians came by.

She was forced into the car and punched.
They drove her to a secluded area,
removed her from the car to the bushes,
and raped her six or seven times.

Juliet S. Kono

They Raped Her

she alleged, six or seven times
in her beautiful green dress.
I was that green dress.

Now,
I am the ghost
of that green dress.
These days,
I float ethereally,
from where the Ala Wai Inn stood,
down to John Ena Road
near Fort DeRussy,
where Mrs. George Goeas,
Alice Araki, and Eugenio Batungbacal—
testified they saw me pass by,
which places me
in the area late that night.

I am the ghost of the green dress Thalia
wore when she said she was abducted
by five "Hawaiians"
and brought to a place,
dark, isolated, desolate,
in Ala Moana
known as Beach Road,
where only a few
small fishing boats
creaked in darkness
and dogs whined,
their cries coming from the old

animal quarantine station.
I am the ghost of the dress
that continues to weave in and out
of the psyche of Hawaiʻi's people.
Then again that's another story.

I am the ghost of the green dress,
iridescent as the ocean
when in the limu's green-bloom,
a green that accentuated
the color of her fair skin
her light, soulful eyes,
rose-pink lips,
and fine brown hair.
To have seen her,
you would have been
hard-pressed to say
she was pretty;
but unconventionally
attractive, she was taller
than most women in the islands
and had a kind of lugubrious
chicness made of old money
and deep unhappiness,
as she walked away from the Inn
in an inebriated sway.

In the car
where she said she was raped,
I don't remember
if I was lifted gently from her legs
or shoved up to her waist
with trembling hands
or pressed by desire
against the heaving
want and weight

of desperate men.
I don't remember if they nestled
their need into my neckline
as they drooled into her cleavage,
if indeed, they even did.

After whatever happened,
once at home,
I was taken off
and hung like a scarecrow
in her bedroom.
She called the police
to say she'd been beaten
and raped and the detectives
came to take her statement,
but Detective Bill Furtado
and his partner, George Harbottle,
did not inspect me much,
as I swayed in winds from the valley.

Only later was I scrutinized,
whereupon they found but a tiny blood
spot and bit of soil. Nothing more.
I remained green, was clean.

I don't know when it happened,
this part folded into my imagination.
But some months later, *if ever,*
I was stripped from the hanger,
and stomped on, in anger.

Torn from across the bodice,
I was dragged out,
taken to the backyard,
where I was hung and set on fire.
Burned in effigy.

Jean Yamasaki Toyama

Burned In Effigy

"It ain't in effigy I wanna burn 'em
but in the flesh, real bones, covered in dark skins.
The papers didn't give her name, jus' said 'a beautiful
young woman, cultured and of gentle bearing.' For
sure she was white and raped. We wouldn't stand for
that where I come from."

That's what my buddy said.
Maybe he's right.

My own blood boiled seeing them
black boys right on top—on top, mind you—
of white girls.
Even on surf boards it still ain't right,
skin on skin.
On the beach they're laughin'
strummin' ukuleles, singin', smilin',
oh, yes, smilin'.

And then those colored girls here
don't act polite. You say hello, they look
right through you like you not even there.
At home no girl treated me that way.

This ain't no dreamy Hawaii,
no joy zone. The movies lie.
Things ain't right here. Color'ds
don't know their place.

We heard the Admiral called them rapists,
sordid people, brutes and hoodlums.
Two of them are even from that orange race,
the one they say we gonna fight one day.

My buddy told me I jus' had no guts because
I didn't wanna go down to the jail to burn 'em.
Then he shoves the paper in my face, "Read those names.
Ida, Chang, Kahahawai, Takai, Ahakuelo.
What are they? Not American."

What We Must Remember

Linked Poems

Christy Passion ▸ Ann Inoshita ▸ Juliet S. Kono ▸ Jean Yamasaki Toyama

CONTRIBUTORS

Joe Balaz writes in Hawaiian Islands Pidgin (Hawai'i Creole English) and in American-English. He has also created works in visual poetry and music poetry.

Doreen E. Beyer was undifferentiated once. She has since then been transformed.

Lynn Cook: INK, those three letters pretty much define my work. Age seven, reading *Tales of the South Pacific*, I was illustrating my imagined island adventures with woodblock prints. Then writing in junior high, high school, and college newspapers—then the thrill of my first newspaper job. "You can use a Rolleiflex, right?" I thought, "Sure I can tell time." What they gave me was a camera. I figured out how to point and shoot. Next stop, creating art inspired by a field of ancient petroglyphs that provide history and images for the next generations. Since that day I have been lucky enough to write about hula, chefs, art, music, faces, and places and Hawai'i's heroes—the modern voyagers like Marques Hanalei Marzan and Nainoa Thompson, who carry our history forward.

Natalia Fernandez is a fiction and television writer born and raised in Montevideo, Uruguay. Upon obtaining a Fulbright Scholarship in 2005, she moved to California to pursue an MFA. Since then, she has worked as a journalist and television writer. Her short fiction has appeared in several literary magazines and journals.

Joseph Han was born in Seoul, Korea and raised in Honolulu, Hawai'i. He is the author of a poetry chapbook, *Orphan* (Tinfish Press, 2015). His recent work has appeared in the Asian American Writers' Workshop's *The Margins*, *The Feminist Wire*, *Connotation Press*, and *Mascara Literary Review*. He is currently the host of Mixing Innovative Arts, a monthly reading series in Honolulu, and is pursuing a PhD in English and Creative Writing at the University of Hawai'i-Mānoa.

Marie Hara: By now each story has so much overgrowth that I cut back as I go. So many memories and stories return to me when I write fiction. I need to cull all the way through. By such attrition, like clearing out a small garden, I might be able to provide some memorable forms, the images of what's left for your recognition and your enjoyment. Thank you to the reader as you follow this. I recognize the pure good luck of your attention.

Retired English teacher **Jim Harstad** continues to submit his scribbles to *BR* in hopes of shaming real writers (e.g. Darrell, Eric) back to their keyboards.

Ann Inoshita was born and raised on O'ahu. She has a book of poems, *Mānoa Stream* (Kahuaomānoa Press), and she co-authored *No Choice but to Follow*, a book and CD of linked poems (Bamboo Ridge Press). Her short play, *Wea I Stay: A Play in Hawai'i*, was included in *The Statehood Project* performed by Kumu Kahua Theatre and published by Fat Ulu Productions. Her creative works have been anthologized widely in local and international journals. She teaches at Leeward Community College.

Lisa Linn Kanae is the author of the short story collection *Islands Linked by Ocean* (Bamboo Ridge Press) and *Sista Tongue* (Tinfish Press), a memoir/essay which weaves the social history of Hawai'i Creole English with personal experience. She is a recipient of the 2009 Elliot Cades Award for Literature.

Dawn Fraser Kawahara, a former Poet-in-the-Schools (Kaua'i), produced her book of poetry and cultural information, *Behold Kaua'i, Modern Days—Ancient Ways*, as a love chant to her adopted home island. She authored the prize-winning *Jackals' Wedding, A Memoir of a Childhood in British India* (a chapter of which was chosen for prepublication in *Bamboo Ridge*). Memoir II is soon to follow, *Burma Banyan, A Quest for Roots*, under her TropicBird Press imprint. The writer currently pens a Monday guest column for *The Garden Island* news, "The Green Flash." Dawn and her husband, a retired biology teacher, live in proximity to Nounou Mountain with birds and books.

Scott K. Kikkawa finds and interviews terrorists, organized criminals, and illegal organic farmers for a federal law enforcement agency by day and writes detective stories from his home in Hawai'i Kai, O'ahu's cultural wasteland, by night. He maintains that a good Scotch whisky goes with any kind of food superbly, or with none at all.

Juliet S. Kono remains busy as ever. Wishes you all to be happy and well, kind and gentle, bright and strong (Mettā Sutta).

Jeffrey Thomas Leong is a poet and writer, born in Southern California and raised in the San Francisco Bay Area. For two decades, he worked as a public health administrator and attorney for the City of San Francisco. He recently earned an MFA in Writing from the Vermont College of Fine Arts, and while there, began a project to translate the Chinese wall poems at the Angel Island Immigration Station. He is seeking a publisher for his manuscript, "Wild Geese Sorrow." This poem is loosely based upon detainee interrogations at Angel Island. Jeff's work has appeared in *Crab Orchard*, *Cimarron Review*, *Hyphen*, *Cha*, and *Spillway*. He lives with his wife and daughter near Oakland, California.

Henry Wei Leung was raised in Pālolo Valley and the San Francisco Bay Area. He is the author of *Paradise Hunger* (Swan Scythe, 2012) and the translator of *Pei Pei the Monkey King* (Tinfish, 2016). He is the recipient of Kundiman, Soros, and Fulbright Fellowships, and recently the John Young Scholarship in the Arts.

Wing Tek Lum is a Honolulu businessman and poet. Bamboo Ridge Press has published his two collections of poetry, *Expounding the Doubtful Points* (1987) and *The Nanjing Massacre: Poems* (2012).

Winner of 2015 AWP Intro Journal Award and the 2014 Intro Prize in Poetry by Four Way Books for his first full-length collection *The Taxidermist's Cut* (2016), and recipient of a PEN/Heim Translation Fund Grant, **Rajiv Mohabir** received fellowships from The Home School, Voices of Our Nation's Artist foundation, Kundiman, and the American Institute of Indian Studies language program. His second volume of poetry *The Cowherd's Son* won the 2015 Kundiman Prize and is forthcoming from Tupelo Press. He received his MFA in Poetry and Translation from at Queens College, CUNY where he was Editor in Chief of the *Ozone Park Literary Journal.* Currently he is pursuing a PhD in English from the University of Hawai'i, where he teaches poetry and composition.

Shareen K. Murayama received her Master's in Creative Writing at OSU's Low-Residency Program. She has published poems in *Bamboo Ridge, The Gambler Mag, Toe Good Poetry, Phoebe*, and *Inter|rupture.* In August 2015, Shareen was selected for the Home School, where she worked with Harriette Mullen. She was also awarded a National Endowment for Humanities grant to study Asian American Film and Literature in New York, attended a Spring Creek Project Collaborative Retreat in 2015, and was listed as a Fulbright Distinguished Educator Alternate for 2016.

Andrew Najberg teaches creative writing and other courses for the University of Tennessee at Chattanooga, where he serves as assistant director of the Meacham Writers' Workshop. His chapbook of poems, *Easy to Lose*, was published by Finishing Line Press in 2007. His poems and prose have appeared in *North American Review, Artful Dodge, Louisville Review, Cimarron Review* (forthcoming), *Nashville Review, Bat City Review, Istanbul Review*, and various other journals and anthologies.

Lark Omura hails from the island of Maui and currently resides in Oakland, California. Her writing seeks to explore the psyches of both locales, and the wide ocean between, contemplating the beauty of being human within the context of a capitalist society. She can be reached at larkomura@gmail.com.

Christy Passion is a critical care nurse and poet. Her singular works have appeared in various local journals and anthologies, as well as in mainland and international journals such as *Crab Creek Review, Haight Ashbury Literary Journal, Blue Collar Review*, and *Mauri Ola.* She has received the James A. Vaughn Award for Poetry, the *Atlanta Review* International Merit Award, and the Academy of American Poetry Award. She co-authored *No Choice but to Follow* and her début collection of poetry, *Still Out of Place*, was published in 2016. She works and resides in Honolulu.

Shandhini Raidoo is an obstetrician-gynecologist and a family planning fellow at the University of Hawai'i. She is a graduate of the University of Oklahoma, and has participated in Writing and Medicine workshops at the University of Iowa's Carver College of Medicine.

Salt, the poet and sculptor, is **Nancy S. Young**. She and her husband live in the back of Kalihi Valley. They feel as if Kalihi Stream has joined their blood running through their veins with the sounds of bulbos, chickens, and geese.

Normie Salvador teaches composition and creative writing at Kapi'olani Community College. Since 1990, he's published his short fiction, poetry, and non-fiction essays and articles in assorted literary magazines, journals, and newspapers. In 2003, Tinfish Press published his poetry chapbook, *Philter*. In his spare time, he's a freelance editor, Warhammer40K miniatures painter, and gardener.

John E. Simonds, 81, a retired Honolulu daily newspaper editor, has lived in Hawai'i for more than 40 years and previously was a reporter for newspapers in Washington, D.C., and other mainland cities. Writing verse since the 1970s, he published two collections, *Waves from a Time-Zoned Brain* (AuthorHouse, 2009) and *Footnotes to the Sun* (iUniverse, 2015). He lives in Aina Haina.

Retired English professor and college administrator at Kaua'i Community College, **Helen Sina** continues writing and teaching violin and viola students. She attended Linfield College, Willamette University, Northwestern University, and the University of Oregon. She has previously published in *Avocet, Prairie Schooner, The Sandcutters,* and *Bamboo Ridge.*

Joseph Stanton has published five books of poems: *Things Seen, Imaginary Museum: Poems on Art, A Field Guide to the Wildlife of Suburban O'ahu, Cardinal Points,* and *What the Kite Thinks: A Linked Poem* (co-authored with Makoto Ōoka, Wing Tek Lum, and Jean Toyama). His other sorts of books include *Looking for Edward Gorey, The Important Books, Stan Musial: A Biography,* and *A Hawai'i Anthology.* His poems have appeared in *Poetry, Harvard Review, New Letters, Antioch Review, Poetry East, Bamboo Ridge, New York Quarterly,* and many other magazines. He is a Professor of Art History and American Studies at the University of Hawai'i at Mānoa.

Bill Teter is still teaching English and coaching the speech and debate team at the University Laboratory School.

Laurie Scott Tomchak was born in Maryland, raised a Valley Girl (it's a long day, living in Reseda) and since then has been freefalling from the Isle of Sark (where she studied the ancient patois) to Puerto Rico (where she taught French) and most recently to the Hawaiian Islands, where she raised two children and now lives in an empty nest in Kailua and teaches Spanish and Linguistics at Windward Community College, Literature and Cultural Studies at University of

Hawaiʻi at Mānoa, and Freshman English at Hawaiʻi Pacific University.

Jean Yamasaki Toyama is professor emerita of French and former Associate Dean of the College of Languages, Linguistics and Literature at the University of Hawaiʻi at Mānoa. Her latest books include a volume of poetry, *Prepositions*, and one of short stories, *The Piano Tuner's Wife*. She is a Beckett scholar.

Joe Tsujimoto has published two teacher texts: *Teaching Poetry Writing To Adolescents* (NCTE/ERIC) and *Lighting Fires: How the Passionate Teacher Engages Adolescent Writers* (Heinemann). He has also published a collection of short fiction, *Morningside Heights: New York Stories* (Bamboo Ridge), was awarded the 2008 Elliot Cades Award for Literature, and was a finalist for the 2010 William Saroyan International Prize for Writing. He is a retired English teacher, open to tutoring and substitute teaching. In the meantime, he is pushing his collection of prose-poems called *Four Gates*.

Lance Uyeda teaches at Windward Community College and co-created its Heroes of Windward learning community. His work has appeared in *At Length*, *People*, and *ZYZZYVA*.

Julia Wieting lives in Pālolo Valley and is a doctoral candidate in English at the University of Hawaiʻi at Mānoa, where she won the 2016 Academy of American Poets Prize. She publishes *Paradise Review* and has previously held editorial positions at *Hawaiʻi Review* and *Vice-Versa*. Her work has been published locally and internationally, with new work forthcoming locally in *Summit*.

Kristel Yoneda is full-time writer and part-time dreamer currently based in Los Angeles, California. She graduated with a BA from George Washington University and has been published in *Bamboo Ridge*, the *Hawaii Women's Journal*, and in the book, *It Gets Better*, based on the popular YouTube movement.

sugar pau!

the end of a way of life